THE NEW
TREASURY OF
GROSS
JOKES

THE NEW
TREASURY OF
GROSS
JOKES

• • • • •

Julius Alvin

KENSINGTON BOOKS
http://www.kensingtonbooks.com

For Miles Lott
and
Duane Swierszynski
and
Mark Daponte

CONTENTS

GROSS

• • • • • • •

Why did the faggot cross the road?

His dick was caught in a chicken.

• • •

How can you tell if you have a high sperm count?

Your girlfriend has to chew.

• • •

What do fags call hemorrhoids?

Speed bumps!

• • •

What do fags call condoms?

Seal-a-Meal.

• • •

What do lesbians do when they have their periods?

Finger-paint.

● ● ●

> There once was a man named Dave
> Who kept a dead whore in a cave
> He said, "Oh, what the hell."
> "You get used to the smell,
> and look at the money you save."

● ● ●

There were three prostitutes arguing about the size of their twats.

The first prostitute said, "My boyfriend can fit one fist up me."

The second prostitute said, "My boyfriend can fit two fists up me."

The third prostitute said, "I don't mean to brag but could you help me off this stool?"

● ● ●

What's black and taps on glass?

A baby in a microwave.

● ● ●

How do you find a fat woman's pussy?

Flip through the folds until you smell shit, then go back one.

• • •

How do you know you're at a gay barbecue?

The hot dogs taste like shit!

• • •

Why do babies have soft spots on their heads?

If there's a fire in the hospital they can carry them out three at a time.

• • •

What's red and hangs off the back of a train?

A miscarriage.

• • •

What's black and white and red all over, and can't turn around in an elevator?

A nun with a spear through her.

• • •

An Amish gentleman and his ten-year-old son visited a shopping mall. They were particularly awed by an elevator. They watched in utter amazement as a woman, stooped with age and walking with a cane, entered the small room where the doors had opened by themselves, then magically closed. Lights began to flash above the doors.

Several seconds passed, when the doors magically opened again and out stepped an absolutely gorgeous, healthy young woman.

The man blinked a couple of times, then said, "Son, go get your mother."

• • •

What is the worst thing about having sex with a sheep?

Breaking its neck when you try to kiss it.

• • •

On reaching his plane seat a man is surprised to see a parrot strapped in next to him. He asks the stewardess for a coffee. The parrot squawks, "And get me a whiskey, you whore!"

The stewardess, flustered, brings back a whiskey for the parrot and forgets the coffee. When this omission is pointed out to her the parrot drains its glass and bawls, "And get me another whiskey, you bitch."

Quite upset, the girl comes back with another whiskey but still no coffee. This time, the man tries the parrot's approach. "I've asked you twice for a coffee, go and get it now or I'll kick your ass."

The next moment, both he and the parrot have been wrenched up and thrown out of the emergency exit by two burly stewards.

Plunging downwards the parrot turns to him and says, "For someone who can't fly, you're a ballsy bastard!"

$$\bullet \ \bullet \ \bullet$$

A wife went in to see a therapist and says, "I've got a big problem, Doctor. Every time we're in bed and my husband climaxes, he lets out this ear-splitting yell."

The shrink replies, "That's completely natural. I don't see what the problem is."

"The problem," she complained, "is that it wakes me up."

$$\bullet \ \bullet \ \bullet$$

THE TOP TWENTY SLOGANS FOR NATIONAL CONDOM MONTH:

1. Cover your stump, before you hump.
2. Before you attack her, wrap your whacker.
3. Don't be silly, protect your willie.
4. When in doubt, shroud your spout.
5. Don't be a loner, cover your boner.
6. You can't go wrong, if you shield your dong.
7. If you're not going to sack it, go home and whack it.
8. If you think she's spunky, cover your monkey.
9. It will be sweeter, if you wrap your peter.
10. If you slip between her thighs, condomize.
11. She won't get sick, if you wrap your dick.
12. If you go into heat, package your meat.
13. While you're undressing Venus, dress up your penis.
14. When you take off her pants and blouse, suit up your mouse.
15. Especially in December, gift wrap your member.
16. Never, ever deck her, with an unwrapped pecker.
17. Don't be a fool, vulcanize your tool.
18. The right selection, is to protect your erection.
19. Wrap it in foil, before you check her oil.
20. A crank with armor, will never harm her.

• • •

What do turtles and blondes have in common?

When they're on their backs they're screwed.

• • •

How did the blonde finally pass her driving test?

She took the examiner with her.

• • •

Why did the blonde get fired from the M&M factory?

She kept on throwing away all the Ws.

• • •

What is the difference between a blonde and an inflatable doll?

About two cans of hair spray.

• • •

Did you hear about the new Married Barbie doll?

You put a ring on her finger and her hips expand.

• • •

Have you heard about the new orgasm pill just approved by the FDA for women?

It comes with a sixteen-inch applicator.

• • •

Two young lovers go up to the mountains for a romantic weekend vacation. When they get there, the guy goes out to chop some wood.

When he gets back, he says, "Honey, my hands are freezing!"

She says, "Well, put them here between my legs and that will warm them up."

After lunch he goes back out to chop some more wood and comes back and says again, "Man! My hands are really freezing!"

She says again, "Well, put them here between my legs and that will warm them up."

He does, and again that warms him up. After dinner, he goes out one more time to chop wood for the night. When he returns, he again says, "Honey, my hands are really freezing!"

She looks at him and says, "For crying out loud . . . don't your ears ever get cold?"

• • •

A gay guy, finally deciding he could no longer hide his sexuality from his parents, went over to their house and found his mother in the kitchen cooking dinner. He sat down at the kitchen table and said: "Mom, I have something to tell you—I'm gay."

His mother turned away from the pot she was stirring and said calmly, "You're gay—doesn't that mean you put other men's 'willies' in your mouth?"

The guy said nervously, "Uh . . . yeah, Mom . . . that's right."

His mother went back to stirring the pot, then suddenly whirled around and slammed him really hard over the head with her spoon and shouted, "Don't you *ever* complain about my cooking again!"

• • •

A man walked into a greasy spoon and ordered a hamburger. He watched as the slovenly, shirtless cook grabbed a fistful of raw meat, crammed it under his arm and began flapping his arm until the meat took the shape of a patty.

"Ooooo! That's gross!" shouted the customer.

"Hah! You think that's bad?" the cook retorted, "you ought to see how I make glazed doughnuts!"

• • •

A woman was looking at the display case in an adult bookstore. The clerk said, "Perhaps you would like to look at our most realistic dildo."

"Oh, you mean one that is exactly like a man's penis?" she asks. "Is it like the real thing?"

"Yes," the clerk says. "After you've used it for three minutes, it goes limp for the rest of the night."

• • •

What is the difference between a whore and a nympho?

Only the nympho will ever use the words, "Please feel free."

• • •

Why is dating so stressful?

Because when you're not getting screwed, you're getting screwed.

• • •

What's the definition of a singles' bar?

Where girls go to look for husbands, and husbands go to look for girls.

• • •

How can you tell when a guy's a real loser?

When his idea of swinging is switching hands.

• • •

What's the definition of bad luck?

Your best friend runs away with your wife.

• • •

What's the definition of worse luck?

Your best friend runs away without your wife.

• • •

Why do men get married?

Most women are very irritating, but as a hole, they're necessary.

• • •

How does a redneck load up the dishwasher?

He gets his girlfriend drunk.

• • •

A young man walks into a doctor's waiting room and sees the only other patient present is an older dude.

"Wh-wh-wh-why are y-y-you h-h-h-h-here," the young guy stutters.

"I have a prostate problem."

"A p-p-p-prostate p-p-problem? Wh-wh-wh-what's th-that?" the young man asks.

"That means I piss like you talk."

• • •

How can you tell the difference between a male seed and a female seed?

You have to stroke a female seed a bunch of times before you plant it.

• • •

What's the definition of bisexual?

Every time someone buys her something, she gets sexual.

• • •

Why do women spend more time improving their appearances than improving their minds?

Because most men are stupid, but only a few of them are blind.

• • •

A guy asks his friend at the bar, "Is it true, Pete, that you now have thirteen kids?"

"Now it's fourteen," his friend says.

"Holy shit! Are you oversexed, or how would you explain it?"

"Believe it or not," the friend says, "I attribute it to the fact that my wife is deaf. Every night when we go to bed, I ask her, 'So, do you just want to go to sleep, or what?' And she always answers back, 'What?'"

• • •

Why do nudists always have the best parties?

On the dance floor, you can see things are really swinging.

• • •

Two guys from Alabama hire a hooker. The first one whips out his dick, which is a whopping ten inches long. The hooker smiles eagerly, and starts to blow him. Then, the second guy takes out his dick, which is only five inches long.

"Who's this guy?" the hooker asks.

The first one answers, "That's my half brother."

• • •

What one word best describes the person sleeping on the wet spot?

Overcome.

• • •

A guy invites a girl home from a bar. As they approach his door, she says, "You know, I can tell a lot about a lover from the way he opens his door. If he shoves the key in the lock and flings open the door, I know he's too rough. If he fumbles forever getting the key into the lock, I know he's no good. What is your technique?"

He says, "Well, first I lick the lock."

• • •

An Eskimo is out one day riding on his snow-mobile. Suddenly, it starts sputtering and smoking. He takes it to the mechanic so that he can fix it. After a few minutes the mechanic comes back and says, "It looks like you blew a seal."

The Eskimo replies, "No! That's just frost on my mustache."

• • •

What's the definition of reckless?

Walking into a Polish pizzeria and ordering one with "everything."

• • •

A young woman who was new to golf was playing her first round when a bee stung her on her leg. She immediately headed back to the clubhouse and ran into her instructor.

"Why are you back so early?" he asked.

"Because I just got stung by a bee."

"Where?" he asked.

"Between the first and second hole," she said.

"Ah," the instructor said. "Then your stance is too wide."

• • •

How can a woman tell when it is time to stop breast-feeding her son?

When he starts selling meal tickets to his friends.

• • •

Why did the nearsighted fly starve to death?

He couldn't see shit.

• • •

The angry wife greets her husband in the early morning hours after he comes home very drunk.

"You've been cheating on me, you stupid son of a bitch!" she says.

"No, I haven't," he replied, "honest."

"Oh, then how do you explain the lipstick on your shirt?" she asks.

"That's easy! I used my shirt to wipe off my dick."

• • •

A doctor decides to inform his patient with the "good news, bad news" routine. The patient asks first for the bad news. "Okay, your daughter got raped, your wife died, your house burned down, your business went bankrupt, and you have AIDS. You'll be dead in a few weeks."

"Holy shit, Doc," the patient asks, "what's the good news?"

The doctor says, "The good news is, there is no more bad news."

• • •

TEN THINGS YOU SHOULD NEVER SAY TO A
WOMAN DURING AN ARGUMENT:

1. Don't you have some laundry to do or something?
2. Ohh, you are so cute when you get all pissed off.
3. You're just upset because your ass is beginning to spread.
4. Wait a minute—I get it. What time of the month is it?
5. You sure you don't want to consult the great Oprah on this one?
6. Sorry. I was just picturing you naked.
7. Whoa, time out. Football is on.
8. Looks like someone had an extra bowl of bitch flakes this morning!
9. Is there any way we can do this via E-mail?
10. Who are you kidding? We both know that thing ain't loaded.

• • •

The doctor performing a vasectomy on a man slipped with the scalpel and cut off one of the guy's balls. Desperate to avoid a malpractice lawsuit, the doctor sewed an onion in his scrotum to take its place.

A few weeks later, during a routine checkup, the doctor asked his patient if he had noted any "side effects" from the operation.

"Well, yes, I have," he answered. "For one thing, every time I piss, my eyes water. And whenever my wife gives me a blow job, she gets heartburn. Last, and strangest of all, every time I pass a McDonald's, I get a hard-on."

• • •

How do they make a lesbian anorexic eat?

Place pussy hair all around her plate.

• • •

One day, after a man had his annual physical, the doctor came out and said, "You had a great checkup. Is there anything that you'd like to ask me?"

"Well," he said, "I was thinking about getting a vasectomy."

"That's a pretty big decision. Have you talked it over with your family?"

"Yeah, and they're in favor fifteen to two."

• • •

A man walks into a pharmacy and wanders up and down the aisles. The salesgirl sees him and asks him if she can help him. He answers that he is looking for a box of tampons for his wife. She directs him down the correct aisle.

A few minutes later, he deposits a huge bag of cotton balls and a ball of string on the counter.

She says, confused, "Sir, I thought you were looking for some tampons for your wife?"

He answers, "Well, yesterday, I sent my wife to the store to get me a carton of cigarettes and she came home with a tin of tobacco and some rolling papers. So, I figure that if I have to roll my own, SO DOES SHE!"

• • •

God and St. Peter are hard at work creating humans.

"The nerve endings," St. Peter says, "how many will I put in her hands?"

"How many did we put in Adam?" asks The Lord.

"Two hundred, Lord," St. Peter says.

"Then we shall do the same for the woman."

"How many nerve endings should we put in woman's genitals, Lord?" St. Peter asks.

"How many did we put in Adam?"

"Four hundred twenty, Lord."

"Oh, yeah, now I remember; we wanted Adam to have a little fun procreating, didn't we?" God remembers. "Do the same for woman."

"Yes, O Great Lord."

"Wait," God says. "Give her ten thousand. It'll be a hoot to hear her scream out my name."

• • •

What's got ninety balls and makes women sweat?

Bingo.

• • •

Did you hear about the two blondes who were found frozen to death in their car at the drive-in movie?

They went to see *Closed for Winter.*

• • •

Where do they put the pictures of lost children on milk cartons in Ethiopia?

On the UPC bar code in the lower left-hand corner.

• • •

How do you get your wife to scream while you are having an orgasm?

Call her and tell her where you are.

• • •

What did the pilot say to the passengers as the plane landed in Arkansas?

"Welcome to Arkansas, please set your watches back eight years."

• • •

What do a bowling ball and a blonde have in common?

Sooner or later, they both end up in the gutter.

• • •

What happens when a bisexual is missing?

They put his picture on a carton of half-and-half.

• • •

Hear about the new device Ford invented that makes cars run ninety-five percent quieter?

It fits right over her mouth.

• • •

How do you know when your wife is really ugly?

You take her to work so you won't have to kiss her good-bye.

• • •

What's the difference between a bitch and a whore?

A whore sleeps with everybody at the party, and a bitch sleeps with everybody at the party except you.

• • •

What do you call a fat woman on a bar stool holding a new condom?

A half-ton pickup with good rubber.

• • •

Why should you feel sorry for people who don't drink?

When they wake up in the morning that's as good as they're gonna feel all day.

• • •

The wife asks, "What do you mean by coming home half drunk?

He says, "It's not my fault . . . I ran out of money."

• • •

What's the difference between light and hard?

You can sleep with a light on.

• • •

Why is it difficult to find men who are sensitive, caring and good-looking?

They already have boyfriends.

• • •

Who makes more money, a crack dealer or a prostitute?

A prostitute—because she can wash her crack and sell it again.

• • •

Guy One meets Guy Two in a bar. Guy Two says, "What have you been up to today?"

"Well, I have been shopping for a present for my mother, who is ninety-seven years old. She is almost blind, her arms shake uncontrollably, and she falls to the floor every time she tries to stand up."

"Holy shit!" says Guy Two. "What can you give someone who has all that wrong with her?"

"A can of floor wax."

• • •

THINGS NEVER TO SAY TO A NAKED WOMAN:

"Cool, I've never been to the Grand Canyon."

"You must be very experienced."

"Remember, you said this was a freebie . . . right?"

"Would you mind rolling around in this flour?"

"So, this is why you're supposed to judge people on personality. It's a good thing you have so many other talents."

"Would you mind wearing a paper sack on your head?"

"Do you mind if I wear one too . . . in case yours falls off?"

"Maybe if I get really wasted I won't mind your body."

"You know, they have surgery to fix that."

"Everybody down at the bar said you were good."

"I expect a good time, at least, the bathroom wall said so."

"I see why everyone said, with you, it's better with the lights out."

"Wow, you like it the same way your little sister does."

• • •

What is the best thing about being a kleptomaniac?

You can always take something for it.

• • •

What's a man's idea of housework?

Lifting his legs so you can vacuum.

• • •

Why don't women blink during foreplay?

They don't have time.

• • •

How does a man define a fifty-fifty relationship?

She cooks/he eats, she cleans/he soils, she irons/ he wrinkles.

• • •

Scott, Brenda, and Phil walked into a restaurant and sat down. All three were absolutely famished.
Scott read a sign posted on the wall nearby. He

then whipped down his pants and started to masturbate furiously.

The waitress yelled, "What the hell are you doing?"

Scott replied, "The sign says—'First Come, First Served.'"

• • •

Why are all proctologists depressed?

Because they always have the end in sight.

• • •

What's more fun than spinning a baby on a clothesline?

Stopping it with a shovel.

• • •

What did the plastic surgeon with a small dick do?

Hung himself.

• • •

Why do women wear makeup and perfume?

Because they are ugly and they smell.

• • •

A beautiful, young babe was talking with her psychiatrist, and said, "Doctor, I can't believe how much you have helped me. I want you to kiss me, please."

"I'm sorry," he replied, "but ethically, I am not supposed to do that. Why, technically speaking, I probably shouldn't even be lying here on top of you naked."

• • •

What is a sure sign that a woman is really ugly?

When she visits prisons to volunteer for conjugal visits.

• • •

What did the dyslexic cop do when he arrested some topless dancers?

He put them behind bras.

• • •

What is worse than ten dead babies in a garbage can?

One dead baby in ten garbage cans.

• • •

On Christmas morning, a cop on horseback was sitting at a traffic light. Next to him was a kid on his shiny new bike.

The cop said to the kid, "Nice bike you've got there. Did Santa bring that to you?"

The kid said, "Yeah."

The cop said, "Well, next year tell Santa to put a taillight on that bike." The cop then proceeded to issue the kid a twenty dollar bicycle safety violation ticket.

The kid took the ticket, but before he rode off, he said, "By the way, that's a nice horse you got there. Did Santa bring that to you?"

Humoring the kid, the cop said, "Yeah, he sure did."

The kid said, "Well, next year tell Santa to put the dick underneath the horse, instead of on top.

• • •

What do men and panty hose have in common?

They either cling, run, or don't fit right in the crotch.

• • •

Why do men whistle while they're on the toilet?

Because it helps them remember which end they need to wipe.

• • •

What do you call a handcuffed man?

Trustworthy.

• • •

What does it mean when a man is in your bed gasping for breath and calling your name?

You didn't hold the pillow down long enough.

• • •

Murphy was sitting in a coffee shop, staring at Jessica, who was wearing the tightest pants he'd ever seen.

Finally, his curiosity got the best of him, and he asked, "How do you get into those pants?"

Jessica looked at him, smiled, and said, "Well, you could start by buying me dinner."

• • •

Do you know why God created man first?

Because he didn't want any advice.

• • •

What's the difference between a feminist and Bigfoot?

One is covered with matted hair and smells awful. The other has big feet.

• • •

What is unusual about maternity wards in Arkansas hospitals?

They include bridal suites.

• • •

How can you tell if a nuclear power plant is becoming dangerous?

The billing department moves out to another location.

• • •

How are fags like killer bees?

Because their leaders are queens and their pricks are fatal.

• • •

Did you hear about the new ice cream parlor run by lesbians?

The flavor of the month is anchovy.

• • •

What is the difference between a lesbian and a catfish?

Catfish don't smell like fish until *after* they die.

• • •

Why did the guy keep a tampon on top of his TV?

To remind him of the cunt that got his VCR.

• • •

What is the chief advantage in being a lesbian?

You never have to sleep on the wet spot.

• • •

A man walks into a drugstore with his thirteen-year-old son. They happen to walk by the condom display, and the boy asks, "What are these, Dad?"

To which the man matter-of-factly replies, "Those are called condoms, son. Men use them to have safe sex."

"Oh, I see," replied the boy pensively. "Yes, I've heard of that in health class at school."

He looks over the display and picks up a package of three and asks, "Why are there three in this package?"

The dad replies, "Those are for high school boys. One for Friday, one for Saturday, and one for Sunday."

"Cool!" says the boy. He notices a six-pack and asks, "Then who are these for?"

"Those are for college boys," the dad answers.

"TWO for Friday, TWO for Saturday, and TWO for Sunday."

"WOW!" exclaimed the boy. "Then who uses THESE?" he asks, picking up a twelve-pack.

With a sigh, the dad replied, "Those are for married men. One for January, one for February, one for March . . ."

• • •

A man decides to have a face-lift for his birthday. He spends five thousand dollars and feels really good about the result.

On his way home he stops at a newsstand and buys a paper. Before leaving he says to the sales clerk, "I hope you don't mind me asking, but how old do you think I am?"

"About thirty-five," was the reply.

"I'm actually forty-seven," the man says happily.

A little while later he goes to McDonald's for lunch and asks the order taker the same question, to which the reply is, "I'd guess that you're twenty-nine?"

"Nope, I am actually forty-seven."

He's starting to feel really good about himself.

While standing at the bus stop he asks an old woman the same question.

She replies, "I am eighty-five years old and my

eyesight is going. But when I was young there was a sure way of telling a man's age. If I put my hand down your pants and play with your balls for ten minutes I will be able to tell your exact age."

As there was no one else around the man thought *what the heck,* and let her slip her hand down his pants.

Ten minutes later the old lady says, "OK, it's done. You are forty-seven."

Stunned, the man says, "That was brilliant! How did you do that?"

The old lady replies, "I was behind you in line at McDonald's."

• • •

How many real men does it take to open a can of beer?

None. The bitch better have it open when she gets it for me.

• • •

What is a Yankee?

The same as a quickie, but a guy can do it alone.

• • •

What is the difference between a Harley and a Hoover?

The position of the dirtbag.

• • •

Why is divorce so expensive?

Because it's worth it.

• • •

What's the fluid capacity of Monica Lewinsky's mouth?

One U.S. leader.

• • •

How can you tell when a man's had an orgasm?

From the snoring.

• • •

Why is air a lot like sex?

Because it's no big deal unless you're not getting any.

• • •

What do you get when you put fifty lesbians and fifty politicians in a room together?

A hundred people who don't do dick.

• • •

A man walked into a therapist's office looking very depressed. "Doc, you've got to help me. I can't go on like this."

"What's the problem?" the doctor inquired.

"Well, I'm thirty-five years old and I still have no luck with the ladies. No matter how hard I try, I just seem to scare them away."

"My friend, this is not a serious problem. You just need to work on your self-esteem. Each morning, I want you to get up and run to the bathroom mirror. Tell yourself that you are a good person, a fun person and an attractive person. But say it with real conviction. Within a week you'll have women buzzing all around you."

The man seemed content with this advice and walked out of the office excited.

Three weeks later he returned with the same downtrodden expression on his face. "Did my advice not work?" asked the doctor.

"It worked, all right. For the past several weeks I've enjoyed some of the best moments in my life with the most fabulous-looking women."

"So, what's your problem?"

"I don't have a problem," the man replied. "My wife does."

• • •

What do you call a woman with a toothpick through her clit?

Olive.

• • •

A woman goes to her doctor and says she wants an operation because her vagina lips are much too large. She asks the doctor to keep the operation a secret as she's embarrassed and doesn't want anyone to find out. The doctor agrees.

She wakes up from her operation and finds three roses carefully placed beside her bed. Outraged, she immediately calls in the doctor and says, "I thought I asked you not to tell anyone about my operation!"

"Don't worry," he says, "I didn't tell anybody. The first rose is from me. I felt bad because you went through this all by yourself.

The second one is from my nurse. She assisted me with the operation, and she had the operation done herself."

"Who is the third rose from?" she asked.

"Oh," says the doctor, "that rose is from a guy upstairs in the burn unit. He wanted to thank you for his new ears!"

• • •

A farmer walked into a drugstore and said to the pharmacist, "I want me one of them thar condoms with pesticides on it. Where do I find 'em?"

The pharmacist replied, "Oh, sir, you must mean that you want the condoms with SPERMICIDE, not pesticide. They're in aisle four."

"No, no, I want me them thar condoms with PESTICIDE on it," growled the farmer.

"Sir," said the pharmacist, exasperated from explaining, "PESTICIDE is for killing insects, SPERMICIDE is for killing sperm. I'm sure that you mean spermicide instead of pesticide."

"Listen here," argued the farmer, "I want condoms with PESTICIDE on it! My wife's got a bug up her ass, and I aim to kill it."

• • •

A prominent Hollywood producer was being ministered to by a talented prostitute. She was giving him a total body tongue job, more commonly known as "a trip around the world". . .

At the same time he was arguing on the telephone with a film director over a plot twist for a new television movie on which they were working jointly . . .

The argument got so heated that the prostitute looked up from her work and complained, "Damn it, man, argue on your own time!"

The producer bellowed into the phone, "We're going to do it my way!"

And then he turned to the girl to bark—"And you, bitch . . . keep a civil tongue in my ass!"

• • •

How is an old lady like Australia?

Everyone knows what's "down under" but who gives a shit?

• • •

What's red and dances?

A baby standing on a burner.

• • •

How can you tell if it's time to wash the dishes and clean the house?

Peer inside your pants . . . if you have a dick it isn't time.

• • •

One day, two girls from Georgia were sitting on their front porch swing. One of them had just gotten back from the big city of New York and was telling her friend all about it.

She started, "You know," with a heavy southern drawl, "they have women up there who have sex with other women."

Her friend gasped, and replied, "Oh, do tell! What do they call them?"

"They call them lesbians," the first girl told her. "And they have men who have sex with other men."

Her friend gasped once again, and said, "Oh, do tell! What do they call them?"

The first girl said, "They call them homosexuals."

The first girl looked around to make sure no one was looking and whispered to her friend, "And you know . . . they have these men . . . who'll put their face in a woman's private parts. And kinda lick around and do stuff with their tongue . . ."

The friend gasped once again and whispered back, "Oh, do tell . . . What do they call them?"

After looking around once again to make sure no one was listening, she whispered back, "I don't know. . . . I just patted mine on the head . . . and called him *Precious*."

• • •

For over thirty years Tony had worked in construction in New York City. Those many years working around loud machinery had taken its toll on Tony's body and he began to fear that he was losing his hearing. . . .

So Tony went to the doctor and told him the problem. He explained to the doctor that things had gotten so bad that he couldn't even hear himself fart.

The doctor examined Tony and then gave him some pills.

Tony asked, "Will these help me to hear better?"

The doctor replied, "No. They will make you fart louder."

• • •

How is a man like a TV commercial?

You can't believe either one, and they both last less than a minute.

• • •

THINGS NOT TO SAY TO YOUR
PREGNANT WIFE:

"Sure, you'll get your figure back . . . we'll just search 1985 where you left it."

"How come you're so much fatter than the other chicks in Lamaze?"

"What's the big deal? If you can handle *me* going in, surely you can handle a baby coming out."

"Hey, when you're finished puking in there, get me a beer, will ya?"

"Yo, fat ass! You're blocking the TV!"

"Y'know, looking at her, you'd never guess that Pamela Anderson had a baby!"

"I sure hope your thighs aren't gonna stay that flabby forever!"

"Damn if you ain't about five pounds away from a surprise visit from that Richard Simmons fella."

"Fred at the office passed a stone the size of a pea. Boy, that's gotta hurt."

"Got milk?"

"Maybe we should name the baby after my secretary, Tawney."

• • •

A little old lady called 911. When the operator answered she yelled, "Help, send the police to my house right away! There's a damn Republican on my front porch and he's playing with himself."

"What?" the operator exclaimed.

"I said there is a damn Republican on my front porch playing with himself and he's weird; I don't know him and I'm afraid! Please send the police!" the little old lady said.

"Well, now, how do you know he's a Republican?" the operator asked.

"Because, you damn fool, if he were a Democrat, he'd be screwing somebody!"

• • •

On the first day of college, the dean addressed the students of the freshman class, pointing out some of the rules.

"The female dormitory will be out-of-bounds for all male students, so, too, the male dormitory to the female students. Anybody caught breaking this rule will be fined twenty dollars the first time. Anybody caught breaking this rule the second time will be fined sixty dollars. Being caught a third time will incur a hefty fine of one hundred eighty." The dean continued. "Are there any questions?"

At this, a male student in the crowd inquired, "How much for a season pass?"

• • •

Two dykes in a bar were looking at a woman across the room. The first dyke said, "Boy, I sure would like to plumb her depths with my tongue."

"No, you wouldn't," said the second. "I know her, and she's hung like a doughnut."

• • •

A man came home from a poker game late one night and found his she-devil of a wife waiting for him with a rolling pin.

"Where the hell have you been?" she asked.

"You'll have to pack all your things, dear," he said. "I've just lost you in a card game."

"How did you manage to do that?"

"It wasn't easy," the husband replied. "I had to fold with a royal flush."

• • •

The New York City subway car was packed. It was rush hour, and many people were forced to stand.

One particularly cramped woman turned to the man behind her and said, "Sir, if you don't stop poking me with your cock, I'm going to the cops!"

"I don't know what you're talking about," the pervert says. "That's just my paycheck in my pocket."

"Oh, really!" she says. "Then you must have some job, because that's the fifth raise you've had in the last half hour."

• • •

A man was out taking a walk one day, when he came to this big house in a nice neighborhood. Suddenly, he realized there was a couple making love out on the lawn. Then he noticed another couple over behind a tree, then another couple behind some bushes by the house.

The man walked up to the front door of the house, and knocked. A well-dressed woman answered the door, and the man asked what kind of a place this was.

"This is a whorehouse," replied the madam.

"Then why is everyone out screwing on the lawn?" the man asks.

The madam says, "Oh, we're having a yard sale today."

• • •

How do you know that diarrhea is hereditary?

It runs in your jeans.

• • •

In school one day, the teacher decided that in science class she would teach about natural resources. So she stood in the front of the class and asked, "Children, if you could have one raw material in the world, what would it be?"

Little Eddy raised his hand and said, "I would want gold, because gold is worth a lot of money and I could buy a Porsche."

The teacher nodded and called on little Sandra. Little Sandra said, "I would want platinum because platinum is worth more than gold, and I could buy a Corvette."

The teacher smiled and then called on little Justin. Little Justin stood up and said, "I would want silicon."

The teacher asked, "Why, Justin?"

Justin responded by saying, "Because my mom has two bags of it and you should see all the sports cars outside of her house!"

• • •

At school, little Johnny was told by a classmate that most adults are hiding at least one dark secret, and that this makes it very easy to blackmail them by saying, "I know the whole truth."

Little Johnny decides to go home and try it out. He goes home, and as he is greeted by his mother he says, "I know the whole truth."

His mother quickly hands him twenty dollars and says, "Just don't tell your father."

Quite pleased, the boy waits for his father to get home from work, and greets him with, "I know the whole truth."

The father promptly hands him forty dollars and says, "Please don't say a word to your mother."

Very pleased, the boy is on his way to school the next day when he sees the mail man at his front door. The boy greets him by saying, "I know the whole truth."

The mail man immediately drops the mail, opens his arms, and says, "Then come give your daddy a great big hug!"

• • •

Why is masturbation better than sex?

Because you can see what you are doing.

• • •

This guy has a pain in his arm and is about to see a doctor, and a friend says, "You should try this machine down at the drugstore. All you do is give it a urine sample, and it will tell you exactly what's wrong with you."

So the guy prepares a urine sample, goes down to the store, puts it in, and the machine spits out a piece of paper that says, "You have tennis elbow. Rest your arm for two weeks."

The guy is thrilled and amazed, thinking this machine will revolutionize medical science. Then he starts thinking, this thing is so good, I wonder if I can trick it. So he goes home and makes a concoction with tap water, some of his dog's feces, and his wife's urine—and to top it off he masturbates into the mixture. Delighted, he goes down to the drugstore and puts in the sample.

The machine churns around for a moment, and then it spits out a piece of paper that says, "First of all, your tap water is hard. Second, your dog has worms. Third, your wife is a cocaine addict. And fourth, you'll never get rid of that tennis elbow if you keep masturbating."

• • •

How do you cook kidneys?

You have to boil the piss out of them.

• • •

GROSSER

● ● ● ● ● ● ●

A guy walks into a doctor's office with a lettuce leaf sticking out of his ass.

Doctor says, "Hmmmm, that's strange."

The guy replies, "That's just the tip of the iceberg."

• • •

TEN REASONS WHY IT'S GREAT TO BE A GUY:

1. Wedding Dress $2500; Tux rental $75.
2. When you retain water, it's in a canteen.
3. People never glance at your chest when you're talking to them.
4. The occasional fart is practically expected.
5. One mood, ALL the time.
6. Phone conversations are over in thirty seconds flat.
7. Dry cleaners and haircutters don't rob you blind.
8. A five-day vacation requires only one suitcase.
9. You can open all your own jars.
10. You can go to a public rest room without a support group.

• • •

TEN MORE GOOD REASONS TO BE A GUY:

1. You can kill your own food.
2. If you are thirty-four and single, nobody notices.
3. When someone forgets to invite you to their party, they can still be your friend.
4. When your girlfriend yells at you for pissing on the floor, you don't care.
5. Your underwear is eight dollars and ninety-five cents for a three-pack.
6. You can leave the motel bed unmade.
7. You can quietly watch a basketball game with your buddy for hours without ever thinking: "He must be mad at me."
8. Everything on your face stays its original color.
9. You can drop by to see a friend without having to bring a gift.
10. Three pairs of shoes are more than enough.

• • •

Murray and Sol, now in their eighties, first met in grade school. Their relationship now is playing cards, playing jokes and making bets.

One day Murray calls Sol and says: "I bet you that mine is longer soft than yours is hard. A thousand dollars!"

Sol replies, "How can that be? If you know any-thing about biology you—"

Murray interrupts, "I called for a bet, not a lec-ture. Mine is longer soft than yours is hard . . . a thousand dollars . . . YES OR NO?"

Sol says, "Okay, I'll take that bet. How long is yours soft?"

Murray answers, "Eleven years."

• • •

A father asked his ten-year-old son if he knew about "the birds and the bees."

"I don't want to know!" the child said, bursting into tears. "Promise me you won't tell me."

Confused, the father asked what was wrong.

"Dad," the boy sobbed, "when I was six, I got the 'there's no Santa' speech. At seven, I got the 'there's no Easter Bunny' speech. When I was eight, you hit me with the 'there's no Tooth Fairy' speech . . ."

"I don't understand why you are bringing those things up," the father says.

"Dad," the boy says, "if you tell me that grown-ups don't really fuck, I'll have nothing left to live for!"

• • •

How did the lawyer get blood on his face?

A mosquito bit him, then threw up.

• • •

How did the necrophiliac introduce himself to girls he really liked?

He would just show up and knock them dead.

• • •

How did the teenager know he had really bad acne?

His dog called him Spot.

• • •

Two army buddies, Jim and Bubba, are on leave and decide to go to Bubba's house to get drunk. Lo and behold they run out of beer, so Bubba says that he will go for more. As he is leaving he tells his wife, Linda Lou, to show Jim her best southern hospitality, which she agrees to do.

Bubba comes back with the beer and finds Jim and Linda Lou screwing right on the kitchen floor!

Bubba yells, "What the hell are you doing, Linda Lou?"

She replies, "You told me to show Jim my best southern hospitality."

Bubba then says, "Gee whiz, girl, arch your back, poor Jim's balls are on the cold floor."

• • •

A little girl says, "Daddy, I wish I had a little sister."

Trying to be funny, the daddy says, "Honey, you do have a sister."

"I do?" questions the confused youngster.

"Sure," responds the dad, "you just don't see her because when you are coming in the front door, she is always leaving through the back door."

The little girl gave this a few moment's thought and remarked, "You mean like my other daddy does?"

• • •

It's a beautiful, warm spring day and a man and his wife are at the zoo. She's wearing a cute, loose-fitting, pink spring dress, sleeveless with straps. As they walk through the ape exhibit and pass in front of a very large gorilla, the gorilla goes wild. He jumps up on the bars, holding on with one hand, grunting and pounding his chest with the free hand. He is obviously excited at the pretty lady in the wavy dress.

The husband, noticing the excitement, suggests that his wife tease the poor animal. The husband suggests she pucker her lips, wiggle her bottom, and play along. She does and the gorilla gets even more excited, making noises that would wake the dead. Then, the husband suggests that she let one of her straps fall; she does.

Mr. Gorilla is just about to tear the bars down. "Now try lifting your dress up your thighs." This drives the gorilla absolutely crazy.

Then the husband grabs his wife by the hair, rips open the door to the cage, slings her in with the gorilla and says, "Now, tell *him* you have a headache."

• • •

What are the five standard penis sizes?

1. Is it in yet?
2. Small
3. Medium
4. Large
5. Nice. Just where do you think you're going to put THAT?

• • •

So a little boy and girl were taking a bath to-gether.

The girl looked between the boy's legs and said, "What's that? Can I touch it?"

The little boy said, "Of course not, you already tore yours off."

• • •

A gay guy hears that one of his boyfriends is in the hospital, so he goes to visit him. His friend looks terrible, so he asks him what all had hap-pened.

"Well, they cut out my tonsils, pulled out all of my teeth, and removed my hemorrhoids."

"You don't say!" the gay guy exclaims. "A total hysterectomy!"

• • •

Did you hear about the town nymphomaniac?

She was so skinny that every time she swallowed an olive, five guys skipped town.

• • •

What is a woman doing while looking at a blank sheet of paper?

Reading her rights.

• • •

What is the best thing about having sex with a homeless broad?

Afterwards, you can drop her off just anywhere.

• • •

A guy goes to the doctor. The doctor tells him, "I'm afraid that I've got some good news and some bad news for you."

"Tell me the good news first, Doc," the man says.

"Your cock is going to get two inches longer and a whole inch wider," the doctor states.

"That's fantastic, Doc! What could be bad news after that?"

"It's malignant."

• • •

What happens when an old maid discovers a cucumber in your house?

She snatches it.

• • •

What are two reasons why women don't mind their own business?

1. No mind.
2. No business.

• • •

Why do women have small feet?

So they can get closer to their ovens.

• • •

What's the definition of a tampon?

A beaver dam.

• • •

What's the difference between a woman and a washing machine?

A washing machine doesn't follow you around for two weeks after you dump a load into it.

• • •

The local priest saw a staggering, falling down, blind drunk come crashing into his church. After picking himself up and alternating between crawling and falling, the drunk finally made it into one side of the confessional. Marking this man as one who was obviously in need of making a confession, the priest hurried into his own side of the confessional, encountering at this close range a terrible smell coming from this new visitor. But the priest steeled himself and said, "May I be of assistance, my son?"

"Well, maybe, slurred the drunk. "Do you have any toilet paper over there in your stall?"

• • •

How do you know whether or not the blonde you slept with last night gave you a good blow job?

The bedsheets are sucked up your ass.

• • •

What is the main difference between a new wife and a new job?

After five years, the job still sucks.

• • •

What is the single most difficult phase of changing the sex of a man to that of a woman?

Sewing in the anchovies.

• • •

Why do women like having their nipples sucked on?

Because it brings out their best points.

• • •

What is the motto of the dyslexics' bestiality club?

"In dog we thrust."

• • •

How is a woman like a condom?

If she's not on your dick, she's in your wallet.

• • •

Why did the banker take the blonde teller into the bank vault?

For safe sex.

• • •

What are the three reasons that make anal sex better than vaginal sex?

It's warmer, it's tighter, and it's degrading to the woman.

• • •

Why don't blondes eat pickles?

Because they can't get their heads into the jar.

• • •

What's the difference between sushi and pussy?

Rice.

• • •

What is a good clue that a boxer is gay?

When he buys his gloves, he selects a purse and shoes to match.

• • •

Did you hear the one about the gay bank robber?

He tied up the safe and blew the bank guard.

• • •

What is the first clue that your marriage is doomed?

When you're on your honeymoon and your wife says you're seeing too much of each other.

• • •

Can you define the sexual difference between men and women?

Women play hard to get, while men have to get hard to play.

• • •

Why are women like credit cards?

Every time you slide it in you know eventually you're going to be out of money.

• • •

What's the definition of marriage?

A ceremony that officially turns your dreamboat into a garbage scow.

• • •

How can you tell if you're staying over at the wrong girl's apartment?

The towels in her bathroom are labeled "His" and "Herpes."

• • •

A lawyer walks into his client's cell on death row, where he's awaiting death by electric chair that very night.

The lawyer says, "I have some good news and some bad news. Which would you like to hear first?"

"The bad news," the prisoner says.

"The bad news is I couldn't get your execution stayed. You are going to fry tonight."

"Holy shit! What's the good news?" the con asks.

"The good news is I got your voltage reduced!"

• • •

What's the difference between a lawyer and a vampire?

A vampire only sucks blood at night.

• • •

How can you tell when an outlaw biker's smile is genuine?

There are crabs in his mustache.

• • •

Did you hear about the morning after pill for men?

It changes your blood type.

• • •

What's a nymphomaniac's worst nightmare?

Meeting a handsome guy with a big dick and herpes.

• • •

Why should you always bury lawyers facedown?

Just in case they come to and start digging.

• • •

How is it so easy to tell when a witch is horny?

Just look at which end of her broom she is riding.

• • •

What is the definition of a real loser?

A guy who gets AIDS from a wet dream.

• • •

What's the ultimate in rejection?

When you're masturbating and your hand falls asleep.

• • •

What is the leading case of death among lesbians?

Hairballs.

• • •

What is the number one sexually transmitted disease among females?

Headaches.

• • •

What should you do if you drop a twenty dollar bill on the sidewalk in San Francisco?

Kick it over to Oakland before you bend over to pick it up.

• • •

How is a blow job like eggs Benedict?

They are both something you will never get at home.

• • •

TEN HINTS SHE MIGHT BE A LESBIAN:

1. Won't stop searching for your clit.
2. Calls your penis "putrid man meat."
3. Strange messages from Janet Reno on the answering machine.
4. Vomits every time you have sex.
5. Has "Lisa" tattooed on her ass.
6. Makes you wear a k.d. lang mask while you do it.
7. Begs you to get breast implants.
8. Gets moist at seafood restaurants.
9. Yells out your sister's name during sex.
10. Tuna breath.

• • •

If newlyweds use K-Y Jelly, what do old maids use?

Banana oil.

• • •

It seems this guy was tired of picking up young women in the bars because they just used him for his money and left. So he decides one night to get the oldest woman he can find. He's been sitting at the bar for a few hours now, and it doesn't look hopeful. But just before he's about to leave, this old lady comes in and sits at the bar.

He goes to work smooth talking her, and after a while she agrees to leave with him. They're back at his place now and he starts kissing her neck and taking off her blouse. Next, he goes to work at kissing her breasts. He gets to the nipples and this white stuff starts shooting into his mouth.

He asks, "You're too old to be pregnant, aren't you?"

She replies, "Yes, but not too old to have breast cancer."

• • •

What is the difference between worry and panic?

Twenty-eight days.

• • •

The housewife got a phone call from the brewery where her husband worked. "I'm sorry to inform you, ma'am, that your husband drowned today in one of our vats of beer."

"Oh, my God! Was it quick?"

"No, it took some time."

"Well, then, did he suffer much?"

"I don't think so," was the reply. "He got out on four separate occasions to piss before he went under for the final time."

• • •

What did the Seven Dwarfs say when Prince Charming woke Sleeping Beauty up?

"Looks like it's back to jerking off."

• • •

How does a deaf woman masturbate?

She gets her nails done.

• • •

Why does it take four women with PMS to screw in a light bulb?

IT JUST DOES, OKAY?

• • •

How do you really know you're from Arkansas?

You think people who have electricity are snobs.

• • •

What's the real definition of gross?

Getting a hard-on and running out of skin.

• • •

What's the definition of an overbite?

When you eat pussy and it tastes like shit.

• • •

What's the definition of a loser?

A guy who gets blacklisted from a bowling alley.

• • •

A woman gets on a bus. As she passes the driver he grabs his throat and makes choking noises. The woman starts crying and hits the driver with her purse. A few minutes later the buzzer goes off and the lady passes the driver as she is getting off the bus. The driver again grabs his throat and makes choking noises. The lady starts crying and again hits the driver with her purse.

A passenger sitting behind the driver whose curiosity has gotten the better of him asks the driver, "What is that all about?"

The driver replies, "Oh, her daughter hanged herself last night and I'm just teasing her."

• • •

What's the definition of "eternity"?

The hour when you come and she leaves.

• • •

How come there are no black workers at Microsoft?

They don't do Windows.

• • •

An older man was married to a younger woman. After several years of a very happy marriage, he had a heart attack. The doctor advised him that to prolong his life they should cut out sex.

He and his wife discussed the matter and decided that he should sleep in the family room downstairs to save them both from temptation.

One night, after several weeks, he decided that life without sex wasn't worth living. So he headed upstairs. He met his wife on the staircase and said, "I was coming up to die."

She replied, "I was coming down to kill you!"

• • •

The playboy encountered a lovely young thing on one of his trips abroad and decided to marry her. Blessing the fact that she was not only a virgin but totally naïve, he seized on the wedding night as a chance to break her in right, and had her suck him off a number of times.

The next day the bride went to see her mother and burst into tears almost immediately.

"Oh, Mother." She sobbed. "I did so want to have children, and now I just know I never shall."

"Now, now, dear, what makes you so sure?" asked the mother soothingly.

"Because," she wept, "because I'll never learn to swallow that dreadful stuff!"

• • •

A man sat in his attorney's office. His attorney looked across the desk at him and asked, "Do you want the bad news first or the terrible news first?"

"Give me the bad news first," he said.

"Your wife found a picture worth a half-million dollars," stated his attorney.

"That's the bad news?" asked the man incredulously. "I can't wait to hear the terrible news!"

"Well," added the attorney, "the terrible news is that it's a picture of you and your secretary."

• • •

THINGS NOT TO SAY DURING SEX:

"Did I tell you Aunt Martha died in this bed?"

"On second thought, let's turn off the lights."

"When is this supposed to feel good?"

"You're good enough to do this for a living."

"Is that blood on the headboard?"

"Is that you I smell?"

"Have you ever considered liposuction?"

"And to think, I didn't even have to buy you dinner!"

"I was so horny tonight I would have taken anything home."

"Keep it down, my mother is a light sleeper."

"This would be more fun with more people."

"Hey, when is it going to be my friend's turn?"

"It's nice being in bed with something you don't need to inflate."

"And to think—I was really trying to pick up your friend!"

• • •

What's the difference between a new wife and a new dog?

After a year, a new dog is still excited to see you.

• • •

Why is pubic hair curly?

If it were straight, you'd poke your eyes out.

• • •

Why do blondes wear black panties?

To mourn the stiff they buried there the night before.

• • •

Why do females fart after they piss?

They can't shake it, so they blow-dry it.

• • •

What is the most tactless thing you can say to a woman in a mastectomy clinic?

"One lump or two?"

• • •

What defines a truly sensitive guy?

He doesn't make his girlfriend blow him after he butt-fucks her.

• • •

What does a blonde use for sexual lubrication?

ChapStick.

• • •

What's the difference between sand and menstrual fluid?

You can't gargle sand.

• • •

What should a guy do when his girlfriend forgets to take her birth control pills?

Give her a good tongue-lashing.

• • •

What do you call kinky sex with chocolate?

S&M&M

• • •

What did the blonde say to the swimming instructor?

"Will I really sink if you take your finger out?"

• • •

How do you know when your girlfriend has been taking too many steroids?

When she comes home, rips your pants down and fucks you in the ass with her clit.

• • •

Why do black widow spiders kill their mates after sex?

To stop the farting before it starts.

• • •

How can you tell your girlfriend is gaining too much weight?

Lesbians start asking her out.

• • •

What do you call an anorexic with a yeast infection?

A quarter-pounder with cheese.

• • •

How many people from Alabama does it take to screw in a light bulb?

What's a light bulb?

• • •

What did the blonde say when she woke up under a cow?

"Can one of you guys drive me home?"

• • •

What is the difference between a woman and a screen door?

A screen door stops squealing after you lubricate it.

• • •

How is a prostitute like a bowling ball?

They both get picked up, fingered, then thrown back in the alley.

• • •

TEN THINGS TO DO IN WAL-MART WHILE YOUR WIFE IS SHOPPING:

1. Get twenty-four boxes of condoms and randomly put them in people's carts when they aren't looking.
2. Set all the alarm clocks in housewares to go off at five-minute intervals.
3. Make a trail of tomato juice on the floor to the rest rooms.
4. Walk up to an employee and tell him/her in an official tone, "Code three in housewares". . . and see what happens.
5. Put M&Ms on layaway.
6. When a clerk asks if they can help you, begin to cry and ask, "Why can't you people just leave me alone?"
7. Look right into the security camera and use it as a mirror while you pick your nose.
8. While handling guns in the hunting department ask the clerk if he knows where the anti-depressants are.

9. When an announcement comes over the loud-speaker assume the fetal position and mumble "It's those voices again."
10. Go into a fitting room and yell real loud, "Hey! We're out of toilet paper in here!"

• • •

Why did the blonde tattoo her zip code on her stomach?

So her male would get delivered to the right box.

• • •

Where do you find a no-legged dog?

Right where you left him.

• • •

Who is the world's greatest salesman?

The man who can make his wife feel sorry for the girl who lost her bra and panties in his car.

• • •

How can you tell you're in a lesbian-run Häagen-Dazs?

They hand you the cone upside down, and it always has hair on it.

• • •

How's another way you can tell you're in a lesbian-run Häagen-Dazs?

The flavor of the month is anchovy.

• • •

TEN THINGS YOU WISH SHE'D SAY AFTER GIVING YOU A BLOW JOB:

1. Gee, that's yummy.
2. How much do I owe you?
3. I'm gonna tell all my friends how great you are!
4. You really quenched my thirst.
5. Let's pop my cherry next!
6. You make a great pacifier.
7. You're so huge, I could barely get you in my mouth.
8. More, please.
9. Oops! I spilled some! I'll just save it for later.
10. I'm drinking milk for good.

• • •

TEN BAD NICKNAMES FOR YOUR PENIS:

1. Old Softie.
2. Warthog.
3. Tiny Tim.
4. The Stinky Twinkie.
5. Limpy.
6. Slowpoke.
7. Two Stroke Engine.
8. Droopy Dog.
9. The Big Dripper.
10. Mr. Syphilis.

• • •

The eighteen-year-old girl told her mother she was now pregnant, and added, "It's all your fault, too."

"How can you say that?" her mother said, "I taught you all about the facts of life!"

"Yeah, but you never showed me how to give a decent blow job, did you?"

• • •

Why are married women always fatter than single women?

Because single women open their refrigerator, see what they have, and go to bed. In bed, married women see what they have, then go to the refrigerator.

• • •

A boy was beating off in the bathtub when his father walked in on him and said, "Son, if you don't stop doing that, you'll go blind."
  "Hey, Dad," he answered, "I'm over here."

• • •

What should a woman say to a man with whom she has just had sex?

It makes no difference. He's sleeping.

• • •

What doesn't belong in this list: Meat, Eggs, Wife, Blow job?

Blow job: You can beat your meat, eggs or wife, but you can't beat a blow job.

• • •

Why does a penis have a hole in the end?

So men can be open-minded.

• • •

What's the speed limit of sex?

Sixty-eight because at sixty-nine you have to turn around.

• • •

What's the difference between your paycheck and your dick?

You don't have to beg your wife to blow your paycheck!

• • •

How can you tell when an auto mechanic just had sex?

One of his fingers is clean.

• • •

What do you do with 365 used rubbers?

Melt them down, make a tire, and call it a Good-year.

• • •

What do bungee jumping and hookers have in common?

They both cost a hundred bucks and if the rubber breaks, you're screwed.

• • •

As the woman passed her daughter's closed bedroom door, she heard a strange buzzing noise coming from within. Opening the door, she observed her daughter giving herself a real workout with a vibrator.

Shocked, she asked, "What in the world are you doing?"

The daughter replied, "Mom, I'm thirty-five years

old, unmarried, and this thing is about as close as I'll ever get to a husband. Please, go away and leave me alone,"

The next day, the girl's father heard the same buzz coming from the other side of the closed bedroom door. Upon entering the room, he observed his daughter making passionate love to a vibrator. His daughter said, "Dad, I'm thirty-five years old, unmarried, and this thing is about as close as I'll ever get to a husband. Please, go away and leave me alone."

A couple days later, the wife came home from shopping and heard that buzzing noise coming from the family room. She entered that area and observed her husband sitting on the couch, staring at the TV. The vibrator was next to him on the couch, buzzing like crazy.

The wife asked, "What the hell are you doing?"

The husband replied, "I'm watching the ball game with my son-in-law."

• • •

HUSBAND: Shall we try a different position tonight?

WIFE: That's a good idea. Why don't you stand at the sink and do dishes and I'll sit on the sofa and fart.

• • •

Gary and Mary go on their honeymoon, and Gary spends six hours of the honeymoon night eating Mary's pussy. The next afternoon, they go to an Italian restaurant. Suddenly, Gary starts to freak out. He screams, "Waiter! Waiter! Come over here!"

The waiter says, "Can I help you, sir?"

Gary yells, "There's a hair in my spaghetti! Get it the fuck out of here!"

The waiter apologizes up and down as he quickly takes the spaghetti away. Mary looks over at Gary, and shaking her head, she whispers, "What a hypocrite you are. You spent most of last night with your face full of hair."

Gary says, "Yeah? Well, how long do you think I'd have stayed if I found a piece of spaghetti in there?"

• • •

How many perverts does it take to put in a light bulb?

Just one, but it takes the entire emergency room to get it out.

• • •

A sailor met a good-looking blonde at the bar and was trying to get laid, without much success.

"I don't date servicemen," she said, "but I am curious as to why you sailors have those two rows of buttons on your pants."

"Why, that's because we have two dicks," the sailor replied.

"Interesting. And probably twice as much fun," replied the blonde. "Let's go to my place and try them out."

So they went to her apartment, and after the first screwing the blonde said, "Boy, that was sure nice. I'm still horny, I want the other one."

Whereupon the sailor undid the other side of buttons, pulled out a limp, weary dick, looked at it and sadly declared, "Well, I'll be damned! He's pouting because he wasn't first."

• • •

Nancy, a rather petite young lady attending St. Mary's Catholic Girls' School, was sitting on the sidewalk, smoking a cigarette.

The local priest walked by and gave her a glare. "Nancy! Smoking at such a young age! Aren't you ashamed?"

"What?" said Nancy. "You know something better to do after sex?"

• • •

What's blue and flies around the room at high speeds?

A dead baby with a punctured lung.

• • •

Why are dogs better than kids?

Because when you get tired of your dog, you can put him to sleep.

• • •

Why do female Jehovah's Witnesses have inverted nipples?

From people poking them in the tits, saying, "Get the fuck outta my house."

• • •

What do women and shrimp have in common?

The pink part is great, and they're better with their heads cut off.

• • •

How do you get rid of unwanted pubic hair?

Spit.

• • •

Did you hear about the fag who had plastic surgery to have his love handles removed?

Now he has no ears.

• • •

What does an eight-hundred-pound gerbil do for fun?

He sticks faggots up his ass.

• • •

This trucker is cruising down the highway when he picks up some slut hitchhiking.

He just gets rolling again and she says, "Pull over, will ya, I need a piss."

"Screw that!" he says, "I just got 'er into top gear; you'll have to piss out the window."

So she winds down the window and sticks her ass out and starts pissing. Just as she's doing it, these two bikers go past and she sprays piss all over them.

A few minutes later the bikers stop for some gas, and one of them says to his friend, "Hell, those truckers sure can spit!"

The other guy says, "Damn straight. Did you see the size of the lips on the bastard?"

• • •

A lady approaches her priest and tells him, "Father, I have a problem. I have two female talking parrots, but they only know how to say one thing."

"What do they say?" the priest asks.

"They only know how to say, 'Hi, we're prostitutes. Want to have some fun?'"

"That's terrible!" the priest says. "But I have a solution to your problem. Bring your two female parrots over to my house and I will put them with my two male talking parrots, which I taught to pray and read the bible. My parrots will teach your parrots to stop saying that terrible phrase and your female parrots will learn to praise and worship."

The next day the woman brings her female parrots to the priest's house. His two male parrots are holding rosary beads and praying in their cage. The lady puts her two female parrots in with the male parrots, and the female parrots say, "Hi, we're prostitutes. Want to have some fun?"

The first male parrot looks over at the other male parrot and says, "Put the beads away. Our prayers have been answered!"

● ● ●

ETHNICALLY GROSS

● ● ● ● ● ● ●

What are the two biggest lies in Poland?

"The check is in your mouth."
"I won't come in the mail."

• • •

A black guy walks into a bar with a parrot on his shoulder.
    The bartender asks, "Where did you get that?"
    The parrot says, "Africa. There're lots of them there!"

• • •

What do you call a barn full of black people?

Antique farm equipment.

• • •

What did the waiter ask the group of Jewish mothers?

"Is *anything* all right?"

• • •

What do you call a hundred Polish girls sunbathing in Cuba?

The Bay of Pigs.

• • •

What do you call a Jamaican proctologist?

Pokémon.

• • •

A Polack on a date, halfway through dinner, asks the girl, "Will you marry me?"

"I think you deserve to know," she says, "that I am a nymphomaniac."

The Polack says, "Shit! I don't care if you steal, just don't cheat on me."

• • •

What do you say when you see your TV floating around at night?

"Drop it, nigger."

• • •

Did you hear about the fag who was half French and half Greek?

He didn't know which way to turn.

• • •

Why couldn't the Irishman finish his song?

He kept passing out after the first eight bars.

• • •

Why don't vampires go south of the border?

Because every time they suck a Mexican's blood, they get the shits for a month.

• • •

Why did the Arab get fired from his job as a taxi driver?

Because he learned English.

• • •

Why did the Polish hit man have to give up sex?

He took out his own cock.

• • •

How can you tell if you have Puerto Ricans living in the house next to you?

Their cockroaches eat out.

• • •

What do you call a nigger with a wooden leg?

Shit on a stick.

• • •

What's the difference between a French kiss and an Australian kiss?

An Australian kiss is given down under.

• • •

How come there were no Australian athletes at the Gay Olympics?

They couldn't get out of Sidney.

• • •

Why do Afghans like to fuck sheep at the edge of a cliff?

The sheep tend to push back harder.

• • •

How many Afghans does it take to screw in a light bulb?

None. They don't need any light bulbs.

• • •

What is the smallest muscle in a kangaroo's ass?

An Australian's dick.

• • •

What did the Polack do when he went broke?

He sold his car for gas money.

• • •

Why do black guys like pussy so much?

Because the inside looks like watermelon and the outside smells like catfish.

• • •

What is white from above and black up close?

A cotton field.

• • •

A Scottish couple was walking across the meadows.

The girl looked at the guy and shyly asked, "Would you like to hold my hand?"

"Uh . . . well, yes," the boy said, "but how did you know?"

She said, "By the gleam in your eye."

They walked a little farther and the girl said, "Would you like to kiss me?"

"Oh, my, yes!" replied the boy, "but how did you know?"

She said, "By the gleam in your eye."

As they got to the stream, they sat on a stump, the girl looked at the boy and asked, "Would you like to go all the way with me?"

"Well, oh, my gosh, yes! But how did you know? By the gleam in my eye?"

"No," replied the girl, "by the TILT IN YOUR KILT."

• • •

How can you tell the Irish guy in a French restaurant?

He's the one trying to decide which wine goes best with whiskey.

• • •

What did the black kid get for his birthday?

My bicycle.

• • •

How can you tell if you're at a Scotsman's stag party?

When a sheep jumps out of the cake.

• • •

What do you call two Mexicans playing basketball?

Juan on Juan.

• • •

What do you get when you cross a black guy with a groundhog?

Six more weeks of basketball.

• • •

What's the difference between a circumcision and a crucifixion?

In a crucifixion they throw out the whole Jew.

• • •

Did you hear about the Polack who bought four snow tires?

They melted on his way home.

• • •

How did the Polish hockey team drown?

Spring training.

• • •

Why don't African-Americans like aspirin?

It's white, it works, and you have to pick cotton to get to it.

• • •

What is long, black, and smells bad?

The unemployment line.

• • •

Why won't Polish ballerinas ever do the splits?

They always get stuck to the floor.

• • •

Why do Mexicans have big noses?

So they have something to pick in the off season.

• • •

What do Polish women do after they suck cock?

Spit out the feathers.

• • •

How does a Jewish American Princess do it doggie style?

She makes him beg for an hour.

• • •

What do you call a black man in Thailand?

A Thai-coon.

• • •

What's the difference between an Irish wedding and an Irish funeral?

One less drunk.

• • •

Why don't Puerto Ricans like blow jobs?

They're afraid blow jobs will interfere with their unemployment benefits.

• • •

What do you say to a Puerto Rican business executive?

"I'll take a dime bag."

• • •

Three Polacks were sitting in a bar discussing their wives.

The first Polack says, "I think my wife is fooling around on me. I went home the other day and found a hammer and a saw under our bed. I think she is screwing a carpenter."

The second Polack says, I think my wife is not

faithful, either. The other day I went home and found a pipe wrench and some pipes under my bed. I think she is screwing a plumber."

The third Polack says, "I went home yesterday and found a cowboy under my bed. I think that my wife is screwing a horse!"

• • •

A nerdy accountant is sent to jail for embezzlement and they put him in a cell with a huge black guy.

The black guy says, "I want to have some sex. You wanna be the husband or the wife?"

The accountant replies, "Well, if I have to be one or the other, I guess I'd rather be the husband."

The black guy says, "Okay. Now get over here and suck your wife's dick."

• • •

Two Canadians are sitting in a bar, getting bored. They decide to play twenty questions.

The first Canadian tries to think of a word and, after a little pondering, comes up with the word: moosecock.

The second Canadian tries his first question, "Is it something good to eat?"

The first Canadian thinks a moment and replies, "Sure, I suppose you could eat it."

The second Canadian says, "Is it a moosecock?"

• • •

Why do Jewish American Princesses wear bikinis?

To separate the meat from the fish.

• • •

How can you tell if an Italian girl is old-fashioned?

She has a handlebar mustache.

• • •

Two Polacks met and one asked the other why he appeared so depressed. "Because I just got back from taking my dog to obedience school."

"So what?" the first Polack asks. "Didn't your dog pass the course?"

"Sure," the second Polack replies, "but he learned to sit up and roll over three days faster than I did."

• • •

What happens to an Irish woman after she has a baby?

She has to prepare two bottles every night.

• • •

Why can't they cremate Irishmen?

Because the last time they even tried, it took two weeks to put out the fire.

• • •

Did you hear about the terrible accident on the L.A. freeway where thirty-seven people were killed?

Two cars carrying Mexicans collided.

• • •

Why don't Polacks count sheep to fall asleep?

Because they want to sleep, not have a wet dream.

• • •

What's the best way to scare off a black mugger?

Threaten to wipe a booger on his new tennis shoes.

• • •

What's the difference between a Jewish American Princess and a toilet seat?

A toilet seat warms up when you touch it.

• • •

What was the real reason the wheelbarrow was invented?

So that black guys would learn to walk on their hind legs.

• • •

What is the most common thing you'd hear a black parrot say?

"Polly want a white woman."

• • •

What's the difference between a black guy and a Polack?

A black guy takes the dishes out of the sink before he pisses into it.

• • •

How do you get fifty Haitians into a paper cup?

Tell them it floats.

• • •

Why are Mexicans like playing pool?

You have to keep hitting them to get any English out of them.

• • •

What do you get when you cross an Italian with a Polack?

A hit man who keeps missing.

• • •

What are the words white people hate hearing?

"We be yo' new neighbors."

• • •

Hear about the Polish twins?

They kept forgetting each other's birthday.

• • •

What's the difference between an Italian woman and a bowling ball?

You can eat a bowling ball.

• • •

What is an Italian concept of a "10"?

No mustache.

• • •

Why don't Arabs get circumcised?

So they'll have someplace to park their gum during sandstorms.

• • •

What goes black-pink-black-pink-black-pink?

A black guy beating off.

• • •

Did you hear about the Polack who couldn't spell?

He spent the night in a warehouse.

• • •

Why do Italian men have mustaches?

So they can look like their mothers.

• • •

Why do Puerto Ricans even bother to get driver's licenses?

Because they come in handy for cashing bad checks.

• • •

What is the difference between an Italian and a monkey?

An Italian has more fleas.

• • •

How can you tell if someone is half Catholic and half Jewish?

When he goes to confession, he takes a lawyer with him.

• • •

How can you tell the redneck at Sea World?

He's the one carrying a fishing pole.

• • •

Why do Mexicans like refried beans?

It gives them a second wind.

• • •

How do you play baseball in Mexico?

Drink some water and try to make it home.

• • •

What's a black guy's version of foreplay?

"Stay cool, bitch. Ah gots a knife!"

• • •

What is a Mexican's idea of safe sex?

Locking the car door.

• • •

Mary Clancy goes up to Father O'Grady after his Sunday morning service, and she's in tears. He says, "So what's troubling you, dear child?"

She explains, "Oh, Father, I've got terrible news. My husband passed away last night."

The priest says, "Oh, Mary, that's terrible. Tell me, did he have any last requests?"

She says, "That he did, Father . . ."

The priest asks, "What did he ask, Mary?"

She answers, "He said, 'Please, Mary, put down that gun . . .'"

• • •

A young hotshot gets a job with the IRS. His first assignment is to audit an old rabbi.

He thinks he'll have a little fun with the old rabbi, so he says, "Rabbi, what do you do with the drippings from the candles?"

The rabbi says, "We send them to the candle factory, and every once in a while they send us a free candle."

The kid says, "And what do you do with the crumbs from your table?"

The rabbi says, "We send them to the matzoh ball factory, and every once in a while they send us a free box of matzoh balls."

The kid says, "And what do you do with the foreskins from your circumcisions?"

The rabbi says, "We send them to the IRS, and every once in a while they send us a little prick like you."

• • •

What do you get when you cross a Caucasian man and a Thai woman?

Syphilis.

• • •

What is the quickest way to make a Mexican forget his English?

Offer him a job.

• • •

If a black guy and a Mexican get into a fight, who wins?

We all do.

• • •

How does a Polish guy do crack?

He swipes his finger across his asshole and sniffs.

• • •

Did you hear about the new Polish abortion clinic?

There's a two-year wait.

• • •

A Jewish family is considering putting their grandfather in a nursing home. All the Jewish facilities are completely full, so they have to put him in a Catholic home.

After a few weeks they come to visit Grandpa. The grandson asks Grandpa how he likes it there.

Grandpa says, "Its wonderful. Everyone here is so courteous and respectful."

"We are so happy for you," the grandson says. "We were worried that this is the wrong place for you."

"Let me tell you," says Grandpa. "There is a musician here—he is eighty years old. He hasn't played the violin in twenty years and everyone here still calls him Maestro! And there is a physician, ninety years old. He hasn't been practicing medicine for twenty-five years and everyone still calls him Doctor. And me, I haven't had sex for thirty years and they still call me the fucking Jew."

• • •

What type of cards do they accept at Korean restaurants?

Blue Cross and Blue Shield.

• • •

How did Miss Puerto Rico win the talent competition at the Miss America contest?

She stripped a Cadillac in three minutes flat.

• • •

How does a Puerto Rican social event review in the paper always begin?

"Among those wounded in the gunfire were . . ."

• • •

What does a bagpiper wear under his kilt?

His wife's lipstick.

• • •

Did you hear about the new sex business specifically for Polacks?

Self-service massage parlors.

• • •

Why don't Italians have acne?

It slides off.

• • •

How can you tell who is the Irish guy in the hospital?

He's the one blowing the foam off his bedpan.

• • •

A Polish family is sitting in the living room.
   The wife turns to the husband and says . . .
"Let's send the kids out to P-L-A-Y so we can fuck."

• • •

Why do black people like finger bowls in restaurants?

So they can wash the silverware before they steal it.

• • •

Why did the Jew cross the road?

To franchise the other side.

• • •

Why did it take the Polish couple six weeks to drive across the U.S.?

Because they kept encountering signs that said, "Clean Rest Rooms."

• • •

How did the Polish woman keep her son from biting his nails?

She made him wear shoes.

• • •

Why do they play sports on artificial turf in Poland?

To keep the cheerleaders from grazing.

• • •

What's the definition of a "fart"?

A Greek love call.

• • •

What is the definition of a Greek?

A guy who believes in enlarging the circle of his friends.

• • •

FAMOUSLY
GROSS

● ● ● ● ● ● ●

What do Christopher Reeve and Catherine the Great have in common?

They both went down on a horse.

• • •

What do Saddam Hussein and General Custer have in common?

They both want to know where the heck those Tomahawks are coming from!

• • •

How is Saddam like Fred Flintstone?

They can both look out their window and see Rubble.

• • •

MARTHA STEWART'S TIPS FOR REDNECKS

1. Never take a beer to a job interview.
2. Always identify people in your yard before shooting at them.
3. It's considered tacky to take a cooler to church.
4. If you have to vacuum the bed, it is time to change the sheets.
5. Even if you're certain that you are included in the will, it is still considered tacky to drive a U-Haul to the funeral home.

• • •

DINING OUT

1. When decanting wine, make sure that you tilt the paper cup, and pour slowly so as not to "bruise" the fruit of the vine.
2. If drinking directly from the bottle, always hold it with your fingers covering the label.

• • •

ENTERTAINING IN YOUR HOME

1. A centerpiece for the table should never be anything prepared by a taxidermist.

2. Do not allow the dog to eat at the table . . . no matter how good its manners are.

• • •

PERSONAL HYGIENE

1. While ears need to be cleaned regularly, this is a job that should be done in private using one's OWN truck keys.
2. Proper use of toiletries can forestall bathing for several days. However, if you live alone, deodorant is a waste of good money.
3. Dirt and grease under the fingernails is a social no-no, as they tend to detract from a woman's jewelry and alter the taste of finger foods.

• • •

DATING (Outside the Family)

1. Always offer to bait your date's hook, especially on the first date.
2. Be aggressive. Let her know you're interested: "I've been wanting to go out with you since I read that stuff on the bathroom wall two years ago."

• • •

WEDDINGS

1. Livestock, usually, is a poor choice for a wedding gift.
2. Kissing the bride for more than five seconds may get you shot.
3. For the groom, at least, rent a tux. A leisure suit with a cummerbund and a clean bowling shirt can create a tacky appearance.
4. Though uncomfortable, say "yes" to socks and shoes for this special occasion.

• • •

DRIVING ETIQUETTE

1. Dim your headlights for approaching vehicles—even if the gun is loaded, and the deer is in sight.
2. When approaching a four-way stop, the vehicle with the largest tires always has the right of way.
3. Never tow another car using panty hose and duct tape.
4. When sending your wife down the road with a gas can, it is impolite to ask her to bring back beer.
5. Do not lay rubber while traveling in a funeral.

• • •

What is the Taliban's national bird?

Duck!

• • •

How do you play Taliban bingo?

B-52! F-16! B-1! A-10! . . .

• • •

What do Osama bin Laden and Hiroshima have in common?

Nothing . . . yet.

• • •

Why can't you circumcise Osama bin Laden?

There's no end to that prick.

• • •

Why did the Taliban stop having driver's ed. class and sex ed. class on the same day?

It was too much for their camels to handle.

• • •

What's the difference between Bill Clinton and Al Gore?

Gore got screwed while the whole world watched.

• • •

What do Clinton and JFK have in common?

Both of their careers ended with a stained dress.

• • •

What do John F. Kennedy Jr. and a penguin have in common?

They're both cute to look at, but neither one can fly for shit.

• • •

Why did Elton John sing at Princess Diana's funeral?

The Crash Test Dummies couldn't make it.

• • •

What's the difference between Mother Teresa and Princess Di?

Five days.

• • •

Why didn't Superman save Princess Di the night she died?

Because he's in a fuckin' wheelchair.

• • •

What will it take to bring the First Family back together?

One more bullet.

• • •

A large group of Taliban soldiers are moving down a road when they hear a voice call from behind a sand dune: "One American soldier is better than ten Taliban!"

The Taliban commander quickly sends ten of his best soldiers over the dune whereupon a gun battle breaks out and continues for a few minutes, then silence.

The voice then calls out, "One American soldier is better than one hundred Taliban!"

Furious, the Taliban commander sends his next best one hundred troops over the dune and instantly a huge gunfight commences. After ten minutes of battle, again silence.

The voice calls out again: "One American soldier is better than one thousand Taliban!"

The enraged Taliban commander musters one thousand fighters and sends them across the dune. Cannon, rocket and machine gun fire ring out as a huge battle is fought. Then silence.

Eventually, one wounded Taliban fighter crawls back over the dune and with his dying words tells his commander: "Don't send any more men, its a trap! There're actually two of them!"

• • •

Why did Jesse Jackson lose the support of black people?

Because he promised them jobs.

• • •

The good news: Jesse Jackson became so successful financially, he was able to hire his own mother to clean house for him.

The bad news: He had to fire her for stealing.

• • •

What do you see when the Pillsbury Dough Boy bends over?

Doughnuts.

• • •

What do you get when you cross Raggedy Ann and the Pillsbury Dough Boy?

A redheaded bitch with a yeast infection.

• • •

What do you get when you cross a Communist with a lesbian?

Chelsea Clinton.

• • •

Why is Chelsea Clinton so homely?

Because Janet Reno is her real father.

• • •

How is getting head from Hillary Clinton like walking a tightrope across the Grand Canyon?

In neither case do you want to look down.

• • •

As part of his parole agreement, Mike Tyson has to go back to school and finish grade five. This is Mike's Ebonics homework assignment. He must use each vocabulary word in a sentence.

1. Hotel—I gave my girlfriend crabs, and the ho tel everybody.
2. Dictate—My girlfriend say my dictate good.

3. Catacomb—I saw Don King at da fights the other night. Man, somebody get that catacomb.
4. Foreclose—If I pay alimony today, I got no money foreclose.
5. Rectum—I had two Cadillacs, but my bitch rectum both.
6. Disappointment—My parole officer tol' me if I miss disappointment they gonna send me back to the joint.
7. Penis—I went to the doctor's and he handed me a cup and said penis.
8. Israel—Tito try to sell me a Rolex. I say, "Man, it look fake." He say, "Bullshit, that watch Israel."
9. Undermine—There's a fine-lookin' ho in the apartment undermine.
10. Acoustic—When I was little, my uncle bought me acoustic and took me to the pool hall.
11. Iraq—When we got to the pool hall, I tol' my uncle, "Iraq, you break."
12. Stain—My mother-in-law stopped by and I axed her, "Do you plan on stain for dinner?"
13. Fortify—I axed this ho on da street, "How much?" She say, "Fortify."
14. Income—I just got in bed wif a ho and income my wife.

• • •

Why does Dolly Parton shop for her bras at Datsun dealerships?

Because her size is 280 Z.

• • •

Did you hear about the new jeans Calvin Klein designed for faggots?

They have knee pads in front and a zippered trapdoor on the ass.

• • •

What do you call one thousand lesbians armed with rifles?

Militia Etheridge.

• • •

Did you hear that Richard Gere is back in the hospital?

He's having a mole removed.

• • •

What has two hundred legs and ten teeth?

The front row of a Garth Brooks concert.

• • •

What has one hundred eighty legs and no pubic hair?

The entire front row of an 'N Sync concert.

• • •

Why does Stevie Wonder have one black leg and one yellow leg?

His dog is blind, too.

• • •

TEN WRONG PICKUP LINES TO USE
ON BRITNEY SPEARS:

1. Do you need help massaging your new breasts?
2. Let me be your "backstreet" boy.
3. Sometimes I wear red vinyl, too.
4. I'm writing my dissertation on your lyrics, and I have a few questions.
5. I'll show you my scar if you show me yours.
6. I've been hot for you since you were a Mouse-keteer.
7. Well, Hel-LO, there, Christina!
8. Baby, I got your big mac right here!
9. Need help with that algebra homework?
10. Hit me baby one more time.

• • •

Did you hear Cher is joining the Spice Girls?

They're going to call her Old Spice.

• • •

What's the best thing Kurt Cobain ever released?

The safety.

• • •

What's more cruel than sending an anniversary card to Yoko Ono?

Sending a Father's Day card to JonBenet Ramsey's father.

• • •

What is Andrea Yates's favorite movie?

Splash.

• • •

What's Andrea Yates's second favorite movie?

Honey, I Drowned the Kids.

• • •

What was Andrea Yates's favorite pastime?

Watersports.

• • •

What did Andrea Yates do to cheer herself up?

She drowned her sorrows.

• • •

Tarzan leaves the jungle, comes to civilization, and applies for a job.

Interviewer: Name?
Tarzan: Me, Tarzan.
Interviewer: Married?
Tarzan: Wife, Jane.
Interviewer: Children?
Tarzan: Son, Boy.
Interviewer: Anything else to your name besides Tarzan?
Tarzan: Tarzan, King of the Jungle.
Interviewer: Jane's whole name?
Tarzan: Jane's hole named "Pussy."

• • •

What do Rosie O'Donnell and football have in common?

Pigskin.

• • •

How do you pierce Rosie O'Donnell's ears?

With a harpoon.

• • •

Exactly how fat is Rosie O'Donnell?

Her charm bracelet is adorned with used license plates.

• • •

What's the definition of saturated fat?

Rosie O'Donnell in a hot tub.

• • •

What's the hardest part of making love to Oprah Winfrey?

Setting up the on-ramps.

• • •

GROSSEST

• • • • • • •

Why did God create women?

To carry the semen from the bedroom to the toilet.

• • •

A guy is driving through the country and his car breaks down. He sees a farmhouse in the distance, so he goes over and knocks on the door. A little kid comes to the door, and the guy says, "My car just broke down and I'd like to use your telephone. Is your mom home?"

The little kid says, "Nope."

The guy says, "Well, where is she?"

The little kid says, "Oh, she's out in the backyard, fucking the old goat."

The guy goes, "Oh, my God! Isn't she afraid of getting pregnant?"

The little kid says, "Naaa-aaa!"

• • •

A brunette, a redhead and a blonde all work in the same office with the same female boss. Every day, they noticed the boss left work early. One day, the girls decided that when the boss left, they'd leave right behind her. After all, she wouldn't come back, so who would know?

The brunette was thrilled to be home early. She did a little gardening and went to bed early.

The redhead was elated to be able to get in a quick workout at her spa before meeting a dinner date.

The blonde was happy to be home, but when she got to her bedroom she heard a muffled noise from inside. Slowly, quietly, she cracked open the door and was mortified to see her husband in bed with HER BOSS! Ever so gently, she closed the door and crept out of her house.

The next day the brunette and redhead mentioned leaving early again, and asked the blonde if she was with them.

"No way," she said. "I almost got caught yesterday!"

• • •

A pregnant woman is in a car accident and falls into a deep coma. Asleep for nearly six months, she wakes up and sees that she is no longer pregnant. Frantically, she asks the doctor about her baby.

The doctor replies, "Ma'am, you had twins! A boy and a girl. The babies are fine. Your brother came in and named them."

The woman thinks to herself, *Oh, no, not my brother, he's an idiot!* Expecting the worst, she asks the doctor, "Well, what's the girl's name?"

"Denise," the doctor says.

The new mother thinks, *Wow, that's not a bad name! Guess I was wrong about my brother. I like Denise!* Then she asks the doctor, "What's the boy's name?"

The doctor replies, "Denephew."

• • •

What's warm and soft when you go to bed, but hard and stiff when you wake up?

Vomit.

• • •

Why do women have foreheads?

So men have a place to kiss them after they suck your cock.

• • •

What's the difference between toilet paper and toast?

Toast is brown on both sides.

• • •

Little Johnny's mother went to the sporting goods store to buy him a birthday present. She said to the man working there, "I want to buy a baseball mitt for my son. How much does it cost?"

The clerk answered, "Fifty dollars."

"That's way too much. How much for that bat?" she asked.

"Ten dollars," said the clerk.

"I'll take it," little Johnny's mother replied.

As he was wrapping the bat, he said, "How about a ball for the bat?"

"No, thanks," said little Johnny's mother. "But I'll blow you for the mitt."

• • •

A six-year-old walks into the kitchen where his mom is cooking and says, "Mom, the last few nights I woke up to this thumping noise coming out of your bedroom and when I look to see what it is, you're sitting on top of Dad and bouncing up and down. Why are you doing that?"

The startled mother tries to recover quickly and says, "Your dad is a little overweight and I'm trying to get him back to normal size. I bounce on him to get all the air out of him."

The kid says, "You're wasting your time. When you go to work, the lady next door comes over and blows him right back up again."

• • •

How does a redneck tell the difference between a cow and a bull in the dark?

He sticks his nose in the animal's ass. If there's a place for his tongue, it's a cow.

• • •

Jimmy went to the drugstore for some condoms.

He went up to the pharmacist and asked him, "Sir, can you tell me where the ribbed condoms are?"

The pharmacist replied, "Son, do you know what condoms are used for?"

"Sure do," replied the boy. "They keep you from getting venereal diseases."

"Okay," said the pharmacist, "but do you know what the ribs are for?"

Jimmy thought for a minute, then looked up at

the pharmacist and replied,"Well, not exactly, but they sure do make the hair on my goat's back stand up."

• • •

How do you give a blonde more headroom?

Adjust the steering wheel.

• • •

How is a blonde like a sailboat in the wind?

When a stiff one comes up, she rolls over.

• • •

How can you tell if your date is Really Ugly?

You take her out to dinner, and the waiter puts her food on the floor.

• • •

What do a whore and a cattle rancher have in common?

They both raise meat.

• • •

"I saw you downtown this afternoon while I was shopping," the wife confronted her husband. "I saw you go into a motel room with that beautiful, stacked, young redhead. I want an explanation, and I want the truth!"

"Well, make up your mind," he said. "Which do you want?"

• • •

How can you tell if it is really, truly cold in your house?

It cures your girlfriend's headache.

• • •

What is a blonde who stands on her head?

A brunette who smells bad.

• • •

Three women had a very late night drinking. They left in the early morning hours and went home their separate ways. The next day, they all met and compared notes about who was drunker the night before.

The first girl claimed that she was the drunkest, and said, "I drove straight home and walked into the house. As soon as I got through the door, I blew Chunks."

The second said, "You think that was drunk? Hell, I got into my car and wrapped it around the first tree I saw. I don't even have insurance!"

The third said, "Damn, I was the drunkest by far. When I got home, I got into a big fight with my husband, knocked a candle over, and burned the whole house down!"

The first girl spoke out again, "I don't think you understand. Chunks is my dog."

• • •

What do a nearsighted gynecologist and a puppy have in common?

They both have wet noses.

• • •

What do you call a tampon used by Nazis?

A twatstika.

• • •

What do you call a fat chick wearing a diaphragm?

A three quarter ton with a box liner.

• • •

How do you turn a triangle into a straight line?

Shave it.

• • •

How can you tell if a girl is a genuine redneck?

When she can suck a dick and chew tobacco at the same time, and know what to spit and what to swallow.

• • •

Why did all the L.A. cops leave the ball game early?

They wanted to beat the crowd.

• • •

What does a lesbian do when her secretary makes a mistake?

Gives her a good tongue-lashing.

• • •

Why don't lawyers play hide-and-seek?

Nobody will look for them.

• • •

Hear about the baby seal's least favorite drink?

Canadian Club on the rocks.

• • •

Why can't queers get auto insurance?

Because they get rear-ended too often.

• • •

What photo do ugly girls carry in their lockets?

A photo of a candle.

• • •

What do desperate girls do for exercise?

Push-ups in a cucumber patch.

• • •

How can you tell if a girl is really desperate?

She sends change-of-address cards to all known Peeping Toms.

• • •

How can you tell the girl you just were introduced to is exceedingly ugly?

You can't tell if your initial response should be to shake her hand or to sniff her ass.

• • •

Why do ugly girls get tired of their sex lives more easily than beautiful girls?

Because for the ugly girl it's always the same thing, wick in and wick out.

• • •

How can a girl tell when her boyfriend needs Viagra?

When she's having sex, it's like trying to stuff a marshmallow into a parking meter's coin slot.

• • •

What's better than winning a gold medal at the Special Olympics?

Not being a retard.

• • •

What does a loser call it when he makes a fist and kisses his knuckles?

Foreplay.

• • •

What is the best gift for a woman who has everything?

A man to show her how to work it.

• • •

How are women like babies?

When they both start to cry they're usually full of shit.

• • •

How can you tell if you are embarking on the perfect blind date?

She comes to the door to greet you naked, and carrying a six-pack.

• • •

How can you tell if a woman really likes oral sex?

She hikes up her skirt every time someone yawns.

• • •

Did you hear about the guy who got his vasectomy at Sears?

Every time he gets a hard-on, his garage door opens.

• • •

What's the difference between a blonde and a mosquito?

The mosquito stops sucking when you smack it.

• • •

A middle-aged guy bought a brand new Mercedes convertible SLK. He took off down the road, flooring it up to eighty miles per hour and enjoying the wind blowing through his hair. *This is great,* he thought, and floored it some more.

Then he looked in his rearview mirror and saw a Florida Highway Patrol trooper behind him, blue lights flashing and siren blasting.

I can get away from him with no problem, thought the man, and he floored it some more and flew down the road at over one hundred miles per hour. Then, he thought, *What am I doing? I'm too old for this kind of thing,* and pulled over to the side of the road and waited for the state trooper to catch up with him.

The trooper pulled in behind the Mercedes and walked up to the man.

"Sir," he said, looking at his watch. "My shift ends in thirty minutes and today is Friday the thirteenth. If you can give me a reason why you were speeding that I've never heard before, I'll let you go."

The man looked back at the trooper and said, "Last week my wife ran off with a state trooper, and I thought you were bringing her back."

The trooper said, "Have a nice day."

• • •

Todd goes to a shrink and says, "Doctor, you've got to help me. My wife is unfaithful to me. Every Friday night, she goes to Larry's Bar and picks up men. In fact, she sleeps with anybody who asks her! I'm going crazy. What do you think I should do?"

"Relax," says the compassionate doctor, "take a deep breath and calm down."

"Okay, Doc," says Todd as he takes a deep breath.

"Now, tell me," continues the doctor. "Where exactly is Larry's Bar?"

• • •

A guy walks into a bar down in the Deep South and orders a Grape Nehi. Surprised, the bartender looks around and says, "You ain't from around here . . . where you from, boy?"

The guy says, "I'm from Pennsylvania."

The bartender asks, "What do you do up in Pennsylvania?"

The guy responds, "I'm a taxidermist."

The bartender asks, "A taxidermist . . . what the heck is a taxidermist?"

The guy says, "I mount dead animals."

The bartender smiles and shouts to the whole bar, "It's okay, boys, he's one of us."

• • •

A flight attendant was stationed at the departure gate to check tickets.

As a man approached, she extended her hand for the ticket, and he opened his trench coat and flashed her.

Without missing a beat she said, "Sir, I need to see your ticket, not your stub."

• • •

THE TOP TEN THINGS MEN WOULD DO
(If They Woke Up and Had a Vagina for a Day):

10. Immediately go shopping for zucchini and cucumbers.
9. Squat over a handheld mirror for an hour and a half.
8. See if they could finally do splits.
7. See if it's truly possible to launch a Ping-Pong ball twenty feet.
6. Cross their legs without rearranging their crotch.
5. Get picked up in a bar in less than ten minutes.
4. Have multiple orgasms and still be ready for more without sleeping first.
3. Go to the gynecologist for a pelvic exam and ask to have it recorded on video.
2. Sit on the edge of the bed and pray for tits, too. . . .

The NUMBER ONE thing men would do if they woke up with a vagina . . .
1. Finally find that damned G-spot.

• • •

THE TOP TEN THINGS WOMEN WOULD DO
(If They Woke Up and Had a Penis for a Day):

10. Get ahead faster in the corporate world.
9. Get a blow job.
8. Find out what is so fascinating about beating the meat.
7. Pee standing up while talking to other men at a urinal.
6. Determine WHY you can't hit the toilet bowl consistently.
5. Find out what it's like to be on the other end of a surging orgasm.
4. Touch yourself in public without thought as to how improper it may seem.
3. Jump up and down naked with an erection to see if it feels as funny as it looks.
2. Understand the scientific reason for the light refraction which occurs between a man's eyes and the ruler situated next to his member which causes two inches to be added to the final measurement.

The NUMBER ONE thing women would do if they woke up with a penis . . .
1. Repeat number 9.

• • •

An old man and a teenager were riding down the road, when the old man pulled over and told the teenager to drive. . . .

The teenager pulled out into traffic smoking the tires. . . .

After the teen came to a stop, he looked at the old man and asked, "Do you smell that SHIT!"

The old man replied, "I ought to, I'm sitting in it!"

• • •

Ethel was a bit of a demon in her wheelchair, and just loved to charge around the nursing home, taking corners on one wheel and getting up to maximum speed on the long corridors. Because the poor woman was a little senile, the other residents tolerated her, and some of the males actually joined in.

One day, Ethel was speeding up one corridor when a door opened and Clarence stepped out with his arm outstretched. "Stop," he said in a firm voice. "Have you got a license for that thing?" Ethel fished around in her handbag and pulled out a Kit Kat wrapper and proudly held it up to him. "OK" he said, and away Ethel sped down the hall.

As she took the corner near the TV lounge on one wheel, Harold popped out in front of her and shouted, "Stop! Have you got proof of insurance?" Ethel again dug into her handbag, pulled out a beer coaster and held it up to him. Harold nodded and said, "Carry on, ma'am, but be careful."

As Ethel neared the final corridor before the front door, Elwood stepped out in front of her, stark naked, holding a very sizeable erection in his hand.

"Oh, God," said Ethel. "Not the breathalyzer test again!"

• • •

Why haven't any women astronauts ever been sent to the Moon?

Because the Moon doesn't need cleaning.

• • •

Why do women have orgasms?

Because it gives them something else to moan about.

• • •

Why is AIDS considered a social disease?

Because it results in a lot of lonely assholes.

• • •

What's another name for a chastity belt?

A manhole cover.

• • •

An artist asked the gallery owner if there had been any interest in his paintings, which were on display.

"I have good news and bad news," the owner replied.

"What's the good news?" the artist asked.

"The good news is that a gentleman inquired about your work and wondered if it would appreciate in value after your death," the gallery owner said. "When I told him it would, he bought all fifteen of your paintings."

"That's great," the artist exclaimed. "What's the bad news?"

The gallery owner replied, "The guy was your doctor."

• • •

How do you know when you are getting old?

When you start having dry dreams and wet farts.

• • •

How can you tell if your little boy will grow up to be homosexual?

He likes to play Lick the Can.

• • •

Why do women have periods?

Because they deserve them.

• • •

Why do women have such difficulty learning to ski?

Because there's no snow between the bedroom and the kitchen.

• • •

How can you tell that the letter you received came from a leper colony?

Because there is a tongue stuck to the stamp.

• • •

Why do women have faces?

So men can tell the vaginas apart.

• • •

THE DIFFERENCE BETWEEN
WORK AND PRISON:

IN PRISON . . . you spend the majority of your time in an eight-by-ten cell.
AT WORK . . . you spend the majority of your time in a six-by-eight cubicle.

IN PRISON . . . you get three meals a day.
AT WORK . . . you only get a break for one meal and you have to pay for it.

IN PRISON . . . you get time off for good behavior.
AT WORK . . . you get more work for good behavior.

IN PRISON . . . the guard locks and unlocks all the doors for you.
AT WORK . . . you must carry around a security card and open all the doors for yourself.

IN PRISON . . . you can watch TV and play games.
AT WORK . . . you get fired for watching TV and playing games.

IN PRISON . . . you get your own toilet.
AT WORK . . . you have to share with some idiot who pees on the seat.

IN PRISON . . . all expenses are paid by the taxpayer with no work required.

AT WORK . . . you get to pay all the expenses to go to work and then they deduct taxes from your salary to pay for prisoners.

IN PRISON . . . you spend most of your life inside bars wanting to get out.

AT WORK . . . you spend most of your time wanting to get out and go inside bars.

IN PRISON . . . you must deal with sadistic wardens.

AT WORK . . . they are called managers.

• • •

Little Johnny was dressed up in his cowboy outfit, and walked into an ice cream shop. Behind the counter was a good-looking, well-endowed, female employee.

Little Johnny walked up to the counter, and said, "Give me an ice cream sundae."

She said, "Okay." Then she asked him if he wanted vanilla ice cream. He pulled out his six-shooters, and stated loudly, "You're damn right," and then put them back in the holsters.

Then she asked if he wanted chocolate ice cream. Again he pulled out his guns and stated, "You're damn right."

After putting all the ingredients on the sundae, she asked him if he wanted his nuts crushed.

Little Johnny pulled his guns out, and said: "Only if you want your tits blown off!"

• • •

Three guys are discussing women . . .

"I like to watch a woman's breasts best," the first guy says.

The second says, "I like to look at a woman's butt." Then he asks the third guy, "What about you?"

"Me?" says the third guy. "I prefer to see the top of her head. . . ."

• • •

One night, an eighty-seven-year-old woman came home from bingo to find her husband in bed with another woman . . .

Angry, she became violent and ended up pushing him off the balcony of their twentieth-floor apartment, killing him instantly.

When brought before the court on the charge of murder, she was asked if she had anything to say in defense of herself.

"Well, Your Honor," she began coolly, "I figured that at ninety-two, if he could fuck, he could fly!"

• • •

The police arrived and found a woman dead on her living room floor with a golf club next to her body. They asked the husband, "Is this your wife?"

"Yes," he replied.

"Did you kill her?" they asked.

"Yes," he replied.

"It looks like you struck her eight times with this three-iron. Is that correct?"

"Yes," he replied, ". . . but can you put me down for a five?"

• • •

West Virginia good ole boy Herman Jamerson went into the army and, on the first day as an enlisted man, he was issued a comb . . .

The following day the army barber sheared all of his hair off.

On the third day the army issued him a toothbrush . . .

On the fourth day the army dentist yanked several of his teeth out.

On the fifth day he was issued a jockstrap . . .

That afternoon Herman went AWOL.

• • •

An eighty-year-old man went to his doctor's office to get a sperm count. The doctor gave the man a jar and said, "Take this jar home and bring me back a sample tomorrow."

The next day the eighty-year-old man reappeared at the doctor's and gave him the jar, which was as clean and empty as it had been on the previous day.

The doctor asked what happened and the man explained, "Well, Doc, it's like this. First, I tried with my right hand, but, nothing. Then I tried with my left hand, but still nothing.

"Then I asked my wife for help. She tried with her right hand, with nothing. Then her left, but nothing. She even tried with her mouth, first with the teeth in, then with the teeth out, and still nothing. We even called up the lady next door and she tried with both hands and her mouth too, but nothing."

The doctor was shocked, and said loudly, "You asked your neighbor?!!!"

The old man replied, "Yep, but no matter what we tried we couldn't get the jar open!"

· · ·

Men are like . . . Floor tiles.
Lay them right the first time and you can walk on them for a lifetime.

Men are like . . . Place mats.
They only show up when there's food on the table.

Men are like . . . Mascara.
They usually run at the first sign of emotion.

Men are like . . . Lava lamps.
Fun to look at, but not all that bright.

Men are like . . . Bike helmets.
Handy in an emergency, but otherwise they just look silly.

Men are like . . . Government bonds.
They take so long to mature.

Men are like . . . Parking spots.
The good ones are taken, and the rest are too small.

Men are like . . . Copiers.
You need them for reproduction, but that's about it.

Men are like . . . Bank accounts.

Without a lot of money, they don't generate much interest.

Men are like . . . High heels.

They're easy to walk on once you get the hang of it.

Men are like . . . Curling irons.

They're always hot, and they're always in your hair.

Men are like . . . Bananas.

The older they get, the less firm they are.

Men are like . . . Miniskirts.

If you're not careful, they'll creep up your legs.

● ● ●

A man was on his first business trip to Japan, and he decided to check out the local whorehouse. He walked in and was assigned a young girl with a body that got him "up" immediately. As soon as they reached the room, he started ripping her clothes off and going to town.

Moaning and grunting, the girl was screaming in Japanese, *"Wasukima! Wasukima!"* He was sure that she was praising him for his good job, so he kept going harder than ever.

Later, he went golfing with his boss and a few clients.

As the clients were Japanese, he decided to impress them with his new knowledge of their language. When one of them got a hole in one, he raised his arms and shouted, *"Wasukima!"*

All of the men looked at him quizzically, and one of them asked, "Why are you shouting 'wrong hole'?"

• • •

After a long night of making love with a woman he'd picked up at a bar, the young guy rolled over and was looking around when he noticed a framed picture of another man. The guy began to worry. "Is this your husband?"

"No, silly," she replied, snuggling up to him.

"Your boyfriend, then?" he asked.

"No, not at all," she said, nibbling away at his ear.

"Well, who is he, then?" asked the bewildered guy.

The girl replied, "That's me before the surgery."

• • •

A man was just waking up from anesthesia after surgery, and his wife was sitting by his side. His eyes fluttered open and he said, "You're beautiful."

Then he fell asleep again. His wife had never heard him say that, so she stayed by his side.

A few minutes later, his eyes fluttered open and he said, "You're cute!"

The wife was disappointed because instead of "beautiful," it was now "cute."

She said, "What happened to 'beautiful'?"

The man replied, "The drugs are wearing off."

• • •

While making up her teenage daughter's bed, a mother was shocked to discover a large carrot under the pillow. When Mary Jo came home, Mother demanded an explanation for the carrot.

"Mother, I want to be honest with you," she confessed. "For the past few weeks that carrot has been my husband."

"Well," the mother replied, "consider yourself a widow, because your husband went into the stew we're having for dinner!"

• • •

Two old ladies were sitting on a bench having a quiet chat, when a flasher approached from across the park. He stood right in front of them and opened his trench coat, exposing himself. One of the ladies immediately had a stroke.

The other lady, being older and more feeble, couldn't reach that far.

• • •

A man was leaving a 7-Eleven with his morning coffee and newspaper when he noticed a most unusual funeral procession approaching the nearby cemetery. A long black hearse was followed by a second long black hearse about fifty feet behind. Behind the second hearse was a solitary man walking a pit bull on a leash. Behind him were two hundred men walking single file.

The guy couldn't stand the curiosity. He respectfully approached the man walking the dog and said, "Sir, I know now is a bad time to disturb you, but I've never seen a funeral like this. Whose funeral is it?"

The man replied, "Well, that first hearse is for my wife."

"What happened to her?"

The man replied, "My dog attacked and killed her."

He inquired further. "Well, who is in the second hearse?"

The man answered, "My mother-in-law. She was trying to help my wife when the dog turned on her."

A poignant and thoughtful moment of silence passes between the two men.

"Sir, could I borrow that dog?"

"Get in line."

• • •

Lulu was a prostitute, but she didn't want her grandma to know. One day, the police raided a whole group of prostitutes at a sex party in a hotel, and Lulu was among them.

The police took them outside and had all the prostitutes line up along the driveway when suddenly, Lulu's grandma came by and saw her granddaughter. Grandma asked, "Why are you standing in line here, dear?"

Not willing to let her grandmother know the truth, Lulu told her that the policemen were there passing out free oranges and she was just lining up for some. "Why, that's awfully nice of them. I think I'll get some for myself," and she proceeded to the back of the line.

A policeman was going down the line asking for information from all of the prostitutes. When he got to Grandma, he was bewildered and exclaimed, "Wow, still going at it at your age? How do you do it?"

Grandma replied, "Oh, it's easy, dear. I just take my dentures out, rip the skin back and suck them dry."

The policeman fainted.

• • •

A man had a terrible accident. His manhood was mangled and torn from his body. The doctor reassured him that modern medicine made it possible for his manhood to be rebuilt, but insurance didn't cover the expense because it was considered cosmetic. So the doctor told him he had three choices—small for $7,500, medium for $12,500, and large for $19,500.

The man was sure he'd want a medium or large. The doctor suggested that he discuss it with his wife privately before a final decision was made.

The doctor left the room and while he was gone the man called his wife and told her their options.

The doctor returned and found the man looking very sad. "Did you make a decision?" the doctor asked.

"Yes," said the man. "She'd rather remodel the kitchen."

• • •

Why are there so many lawyers in the U.S.?

Because St. Patrick chased the snakes out of Ireland.

• • •

Where do vampires learn to suck blood?

Law school.

• • •

Why is eight years old considered an awkward age for a boy?

He's too old to suck on his mother's tit and too young to suck on anyone else's.

• • •

How can a kid tell when his parents hate him?

When he sets the house on fire, he gets sent to his room.

• • •

What do you get when you offer a blonde a penny for her thoughts?

A refund.

• • •

What's the difference between a blonde and a Porsche?

You can only fit two people in a Porsche.

• • •

What is another name for a queer sixty-nine?

A doubleheader.

• • •

What do blondes and screen doors have in common?

The harder you slam them, the looser they get.

• • •

What did the blonde's mom say to her before she went out?

If you're not in bed by midnight, come home.

• • •

How many blondes does it take to screw in a light-bulb?

None. They screw in cars.

• • •

DRINKING AGE

Seventeen: beer
Twenty-five: vodka
Thirty-five: scotch
Forty-eight: double scotch
Sixty-six: Mylanta

• • •

What's the difference between oral and rectal ther-mometers?

The taste.

• • •

Did you hear about the dyslexic Satanist?

He sold his soul to Santa.

• • •

TEN WRONG THINGS TO SAY WHEN YOU
CAN'T GET IT UP:
1. Must be sunspots.
2. I'm too tired from banging my secretary.
3. My pump blew a gasket.
4. If you turn the game on, I'm sure it will rise.
5. I forgot to fill my prescription.
6. I guess this means you don't really love me.
7. I dunno, worked fine with your sister.
8. I just want to satisfy you, baby.
9. Oops . . . I already came.
10. I guess the stench killed him.

• • •

What is a seventy-two?

Sixty-nine with a five percent meal tax.

• • •

Did you hear about the blonde whose boyfriend told her he loved her?

She believed him.

• • •

How do you get a man to do sit-ups?

Glue the TV remote between his ankles.

• • •

What is grosser than gross?

When you wake up in a strange bed one morning and find a lump in your throat, then realize that there's a string attached to it.

• • •

Why do women have babies?

Because it hurts and they deserve it.

• • •

Why can't Italian men give their wives mink coats?

Because the fur clashes with their wives' moustaches.

• • •

How do Eskimos give birth?

They start out by rubbing noses, and pretty soon the little buggers fall out.

• • •

How do you make Italian sausage?

From retarded pigs.

• • •

Why is it traditional to boil water when a woman is giving birth to a baby?

Because if the baby dies, you can make soup.

• • •

A blonde goes to see her doctor because of serious abrasions on her knees.

"Do you know what caused these injuries?" the doctor asks.

"Well," she replies, "I've been having sex doggie style."

"Oh, that's no problem," the doctor says. "Just roll over and do it missionary style for a while."

"Oh, but that is a problem," the blonde says. "Every time I try it that way, my dog's breath makes me puke!"

• • •

Two gay guys are in a hot tub pushing a big turd back and forth in the water. Another guy walks by and asks, "What the hell are you two doing?"

The first fag replies, "We're teaching our baby how to swim!"

• • •

Why did the feminist commit suicide?

She saw herself in the mirror.

• • •

What's the definition of gross?

Grandpa giving Grandma a hickey and the skin pops.

• • •

A homeless person walks into a bar. He asks the barman for a cocktail stick. The barman, being a nice guy, gives the man a cocktail stick. The guy thanks him and leaves.

A couple of minutes later, another homeless guy comes in and asks for a cocktail stick. The barman, getting rather confused, gives him one and watches him leave.

A third homeless guy comes in and asks for the same thing.

A fourth homeless guy comes in and asks for a straw. The barman asks, "Don't you want a cock-tail stick like all the others?"

The fourth homeless guy says, "No, thanks. Someone was sick outside and all the lumpy bits have gone!"

• • •

Two fags were walking down the street and passed a handsome guy. One fag turned to the other and said, "See that stud there, Bruce?"

"Sure," said the second fag.

"Well, let me tell you, he's a tremendous fuck," the first fag said.

"No shit?" his friend asked.

The first fag replied, "Well, hardly any."

• • •

What is black and has twelve green tits?

The garbage bag at a breast cancer clinic.

• • •

What's the definition of disgusting?

Stuffing a dozen oysters into an old lady's cunt and sucking out thirteen.

• • •

What's a man's definition of a romantic evening?

Sex.

• • •

How can a girl tell if her date is a real loser?

His teddy bear is equipped with a vagina.

• • •

What's worse than a male chauvinist pig?

A woman that won't do what she's told.

• • •

Why do men want to vote for a female for president?

Because we'd only have to pay her half as much.

• • •

"I'm afraid I have some good news and some bad news," the doctor says to the female patient.

"Well, give me the good news first, Doc," she says.

The doctor replies, "Your lab tests came back today, and your crabs are all gone."

She says, "Gee, that's great! But what's the bad news?"

The doctor tells her, "We don't know what killed them."

• • •

How can a redneck tell if he had a good time at the party last night?

He wakes up in a pool of his own puke.

• • •

A guy's on the electric chair. The warden's just about to pull the switch when the guy gets the hiccups.

The warden says, "Do you have any last requests?"

The guy says, "*Hic* . . . Yeah . . . could you please do *hic* . . . could you please do . . . *hic* . . . something to scare me?"

• • •

A guy goes in to see a psychiatrist. He says, "Doc, I can't seem to make any friends. Can you help me, you fat slob?"

• • •

FIVE THINGS YOU SHOULD NEVER SAY IN
A MEN'S ROOM:

1. "Interesting . . . more floaters than sinkers."
2. "I've never seen that color before."
3. "Damn, this water's cold."
4. "Boy, that sure looks like a maggot."
5. "Whew! Who died?"

• • •

Little Johnny is late to class one day and the teacher asks him where he has been.

He replies, "I've been down by the creek sticking cherry bombs up frogs' asses."

"You mean 'rectum,'" corrects the teacher.

"Wrecked 'em?" says little Johnny, "I fuckin' *killed* 'em!"

• • •

Two old women were sitting on a bench waiting for their bus. The buses were running late, and a lot of time passed. Finally, one woman turned to the other and said, "You know, I've been sitting here so long, my butt fell asleep!"

The other woman turned to her and said, "I know! I heard it snoring!"

• • •

Grossest

How can you tell if a whore is genuinely elegant?

She uses lipstick on all of her VD sores.

• • •

THE TEN SIGNS YOU DRINK TOO MUCH:

1. The back of your head keeps getting hit by the toilet seat.
2. You lose arguments with inanimate objects.
3. You can focus better with one eye closed.
4. Boris Yeltsin called personally to ask you to slow down on the vodka.
5. Worried friends call Monday morning to make sure you returned the goat.
6. You fart and then feel a lump in your back pocket.
7. You don't recognize your wife unless seen through the bottom of a glass.
8. That damned pink elephant followed you home again.
9. You have to hold onto the lawn to keep from falling off the earth.
10. You fall off the floor.

• • •